# Donne's Poetry and Modern Criticism

# Donne's Poetry
# and
# Modern Criticism

*Leonard Unger*

*New York*
RUSSELL & RUSSELL

TO

AUSTIN WARREN

and

RENÉ WELLEK

and to the years

1939–1941

# CONTENTS

# Introduction

🝄

THIS ESSAY was written in 1941. I have changed only a few words and phrases here and there and have refrained from any attempt to impose on it a strictly up-to-date appearance. The purpose of the essay and whatever value it may have are not, I believe, affected by the passage of a few years. The issues raised in it are among those which are still debated and explored, and it is likely that they will continue to be issues of critical preoccupation.

In the opening sentence of the essay I observed that the word *metaphysical* is a frequent term in modern criticism—a statement I would hesitate to make about the criticism of poetry written in the nineteen-forties. But I did not hesitate to make it about the thirties and earlier, and the criticism of that period is still, I presume, modern. It would probably be more accurate to say that it is contemporary, in that the discussions by Grierson, Eliot, Ransom, Tate, Brooks and other critics have a current and vital function as critical comment on the poetry of John Donne and the subject of metaphysical poetry, as well as in the more general field of poetic theory. These discussions have provided concepts and terms that are elements in prevalent and established attitudes. The critics have continued to pursue their studies, in some cases to develop and alter their ideas; and their earlier preoccupation with Donne and their use of *metaphysical* have been the point from which they have developed.

For example, for his second book of criticism Cleanth Brooks takes his title, *The Well Wrought Urn,* from John

Donne, and discusses his work at some length toward the beginning and end of the book, although there is otherwise no apparent emphasis on Donne nor a particular concept of metaphysical poetry. A significant difference between Brooks' two books may be conveniently indicated by a glance at their indices. In the index to the earlier book, *Modern Poetry and the Tradition*, there are numerous page references under *metaphysical*, while that term does not appear at all in the index to *The Well Wrought Urn*. On the other hand, the earlier book has no index entry for *paradox*, a term frequently used in the later book, as its index shows. (Incidentally, some of my conclusions in this essay are, so far as Donne is concerned, in close accord with Brooks' notions of paradox.)

A similar comparison may be made of Ransom's two books. The earlier of these, *The World's Body*, has no index, but I recall that *metaphysical* is used with some frequency, and that what the term signified for Ransom is even more frequently suggested and implied. In *The New Criticism*, according to the index, *metaphysical* is used only in the discussion of Eliot's essay, "The Metaphysical Poets," and although it is not clearly reflected by the index, I find that in *The New Criticism* the terms *logical* and *ontological* more readily represent the tendency of Ransom's thought. There is some similarity in the development (or extension) of the critical thought of both Ransom and Brooks. Each critic has moved away from more narrowly formulaic principles toward greater preoccupation with the conceptual and attitudinal, although in each case the continuity of their thought from the earlier, "metaphysical" position is obvious enough and could be easily demonstrated.

Some of the critical issues pursued in this essay are similar to those raised by Rosemond Tuve in her monumental *Elizabethan and Metaphysical Imagery*—especially in those footnotes and appendices where she often cites the same critics and pronouncements that I do. (See the index to her book.) Much that has been vague and questionable in comment on the subject is clarified by her searching scholarship. She reconstructs the formal rhetoric and logic of the times and shows how these disciplines affected the course of poetry from Spenser to Dryden. She stresses what poets were consciously doing with images and what readers must have expected from and seen in their performances. This emphasis on the general point of view has led Miss Tuve to treat numerous brief passages from many poets throughout the period studied rather than whole poems or groups of whole poems by a single poet. There is, consequently, less attention to what distinguishes the individual poet, and more to the characteristics common to all poets within the period.

Modern criticism, which has probably stirred Miss Tuve to her rewarding labors, can take a large benefit from her achievement. At the same time, it is neither likely nor desirable that speculation about Elizabethan and metaphysical imagery will be put to rest by her book. The modern critic wants not only to reconstruct the ideas of a past era concerning the craft of poetry, but also to translate those ideas into modern terms and modern significances. He wants to move beyond the scholar's reconstruction and proceed from what was conscious and obvious for the past to an insight into what was inherent and probably unconscious. Finally, he wants to relate literature not only to the general attitudes by and for which it was produced, but to the attitudes for which it survives. This is the purpose of the critics whom I discuss, and if I have taken issue with them, it is because I wished to join them in that purpose.

Grateful acknowledgment is made to the following authors, publishers and holders of copyright for permission to reprint passages from their writings and publications:

The Clarendon Press, Oxford, England: the Introduction to *Metaphysical Lyrics and Poems of the Seventeenth Century*, edited by Sir Herbert Grierson.

Harcourt, Brace & Company, New York: *Selected Essays* by T. S. Eliot.

Harvard University Press, Cambridge: *The Donne Tradition* by George Williamson.

Mr. W. R. Moses: *The Metaphysical Conceit in the Poems of John Donne* (doctoral dissertation), Vanderbilt University, Nashville, Tenn.

Mr. John Crowe Ransom and Charles Scribner's Sons, New York: *The World's Body* by John Crowe Ransom.

Mr. Allen Tate and William Morrow & Company, New York: *On the Limits of Poetry* by Allen Tate.

The University of North Carolina Press, Chapel Hill: *Modern Poetry and the Tradition* by Cleanth Brooks.

# Donne's Poetry and Modern Criticism

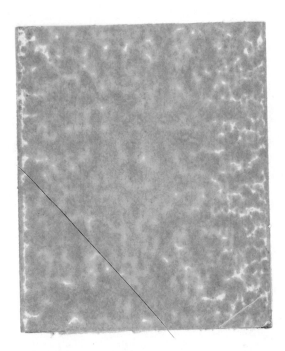

# Chapter I

## THE CRITICS

### Modern Definitions of "Metaphysical"

It is my impression that in modern criticism of poetry the word *metaphysical* has been used more frequently than any other comparable term—if there is one comparable. The term has become, moreover, categorial in a way for a body of modern critical theory and the contemporary poetic practice associated with that theory. Yet, if this word suggests a category, it is a very loose one. My intention is to examine some of the criticism employing the word and some of the literature embraced by it, to make the category tighter and clearer, or else to discover that it is unfit for categorial pretension—at least beyond its historical origin.

As a result of Dryden's reference to Donne as "affecting the metaphysic" and more particularly of Dr. Johnson's naming as "metaphysical" Donne and the seventeenth-century poets showing his influence, historians of English literature have persistently used the term for grouping together certain poets of the seventeenth century. Modern critics, passing favorable judgment upon the work of these poets, often use the term to imply—and even make explicit —an aesthetic formula by which a kind of poetry may have been written before or since the time of Donne and his immediate followers. One finds critics writing the word

3

*metaphysical* with a capital letter, in italics, or within quotation marks. This suggests that they do not always mean simply what the philosophers have meant by it. And a survey of their writings finds the term used with no consistent significance throughout, at times with a lack of clarity, and often in questionable propositions.

## H. J. C. GRIERSON

A review of comment upon metaphysical poetry may well begin with Sir Herbert Grierson, the foremost editor of Donne and one of the earliest in this century to write admiringly upon the subject. Introducing his edition of *Metaphysical Lyrics and Poems of the Seventeenth Century,* Grierson uses *metaphysical* in its customary philosophic meaning: he says that metaphysical poetry was written by Lucretius, Dante, and Goethe; that it is poetry that "has been inspired by a philosophical conception of the universe and the role assigned to the human spirit in the great drama of existence." [1] This definition could certainly be applied to poetry (e.g., Shelley's *Prometheus Unbound*) with which that of the seventeenth century is often contrasted. Donne and his followers wrote poems of no such proportions, were metaphysical in not so large a way, yet Grierson finds it especially adequate to call them metaphysical. His characterization of the poetry, to show the justness of the title given it, deserves quotation, for we find echoes of it and statements of a similar nature in the discussions of later writers. The term *metaphysical*

lays stress on all the right things—the survival, one might say the reaccentuation, of the metaphysical strain, the *concetti metafisici ed ideali* as Testi calls them in contrast to the simpler imagery of classical poetry, of mediaeval Italian poetry; the more intellectual, less verbal, character of their wit compared with the conceits of the Elizabethans; the finer psychology of which their conceits are often the expression; their learned imagery; the argumentative, subtle evolution of their lyrics;

4

above all the peculiar blend of passion and thought, feeling and ratiocination which is their greatest achievement. Passionate thinking is always apt to become metaphysical, probing and investigating the experience from which it takes its rise. All these qualities are in the poetry of Donne, and Donne is the greatest master of English poetry in the seventeenth century.[2]

Grierson's remarks are certainly instructive, and one has faith in the soundness of his historical references; yet one could wish that his statements were developed from analyses of particular poems, or that his own propositions were always such that they could be analyzed with reference to particular poems. Expressions like "blend of passion and thought" and "passionate thinking" may well suggest the quality of one's experience upon reading the poetry, and they might reasonably be used in making good guesses about the minds of the authors, but they can hardly be used for discussing the structure of a poem or a poetic method. What Grierson says may seem, for readers of Donne, to follow from the poetry, and he has been repeated in one way and another by several writers since his essay appeared. But if this poetry is to be distinguished from other kinds, it would be well to follow impressionistic statements with analysis of the poetry in terms that refer to the poetry, not the poet's hypothetical personality or a reader's private articulate response. The phrase "passionate thinking" can convey but little knowledge to us when even the psychologists are not satisfied with their understanding of passion and thinking; how such thinking becomes metaphysical cannot be less mysterious than the thinking itself. Grierson's mention of "wit" and "conceits" is the beginning of the kind of definition that is desirable, if possible (i.e., a "public" or structural account), and we shall attend more fully to these matters in a treatment of the comment made by other writers.

# T. S. ELIOT

T. S. Eliot, whose essay "The Metaphysical Poets" was written as a review of the book edited by Grierson, is generally acknowledged to be largely responsible for the growth of popular and critical interest in metaphysical poetry. He, too, discusses the reader's experience and the psychological constitution of the poets. This he does with many quotations and remarks that suggest a genuine appreciation, an appreciation and delicacy of feeling which many readers have found contagious, which have stimulated many practicing poets. And one suspects that Eliot is quite aware of what he is doing. He does not argue that the term *metaphysical* in its philosophical sense is an apt description of the poetry nor does he cut the term loose from its historical moorings, as Grierson partly does, and as some later critics emphatically do. When he turns to a characteristic structural problem he makes an observation which may be the only structural generalization a close study of the poetry can yield:

It is difficult to find any precise use of metaphor, simile, or other conceit, which is common to all the poets and at the same time important enough to isolate these poets as a group. Donne, and often Cowley, employ a device which is sometimes considered characteristically "metaphysical"; the elaboration (contrasted with the condensation) of a figure of speech to the farthest stage to which ingenuity can carry it.[3]

It should be noticed that Eliot does not raise the question of value in mentioning the characteristic elements of the poetry; in this he is more cautious than other critics. He gives a definition of the conceit which agrees with the *discordia concors* that Dr. Johnson saw in it; and he does not, as other critics have done, place the conceit topmost upon a hierarchical scale of poetic devices: "The conceit itself is primarily an eccentricity of imagery, the farfetched association of the dissimilar, or the overelaboration of one metaphor or simile."[4] Nevertheless, there are many state-

6

ments in Eliot's essays similar to the expression about the combination of thought and feeling; and later critics have borrowed his phrases and used them as if they were propositions having reference to the structural aspects of a poem:

In Chapman especially there is a direct sensuous apprehension of thought, or a re-creation of thought into feeling, which is exactly what we find in Donne.[5]

Tennyson and Browning are poets, and they think; but they do not feel their thought as immediately as the odour of a rose.[6]

One may be curious to know how the seventeenth-century poets used language that these things can be said of them with more justice than of Milton, Wordsworth, Shelley, and Browning—if someone wanted to argue that these later poets were unrivaled "passionate thinkers," and so on. Since it reappears in the writings of others, it should be pointed out that the expression "a tough reasonableness beneath the slight lyric grace," [7] which Eliot puts in apposition with Marvell's wit, tells us nothing about the wit or the poetry, although it may intimate the quality of one's feelings (Eliot's, originally) about these. At any rate, with *wit* and what is meant by a *conceit*, we are moving closer to the poetry and are being provided with propositions that can be tested by poems.

## GEORGE WILLIAMSON

*The Donne Tradition* by George Williamson springs, as the author acknowledges, from the suggestions and statements of T. S. Eliot. Mr. Williamson discusses the seventeenth-century group of poets called metaphysical, with special attention to John Donne as the founder and supreme example of a certain way of writing poetry. There is much in the book concerning what Mr. Eliot had called the unified sensibility of the seventeenth century, with considerable imaginative ramification by Mr. Williamson on the nature of this sensibility. And there are extended and frequent discussions of wit and the conceit, and comments on particular passages of poetry, mostly in phrases that are variations of the *combination of thought and feeling*.

It is in such combination (of the ingenious and the imaginative) that the conceit attains to high poetic value; the idea and the figure become one, and we have Donne's *Valediction*, King's *Exequy*, Herbert's *Pulley*, or Marvell's *Coy Mistress* . . . for these poems are moving and sincere.[8]

Mr. Eliot's phraseology on the minds of the poets echoes and re-echoes through the book. Mr. Williamson's habit is to use, as counters for recording his feelings about the poetry, expressions invented by Mr. Eliot; his remarks are indeed witness to the suggestibility of the poetry. We are, however, left curious to know what a conceit is doing in and to a poem, in addition to its effect upon the reader:

The expanded conceit is successful when the idea and the figure become one, and the condensed conceit when the image is the very body of the thought. Thus we see the close relation of the conceit to the sensuous thinking of Donne which I have already described. The conceit, playing like the shuttle between his mind and the world, wove the fabric of the thought, and gave the pattern in which he united his most disparate knowledge and experience into an image witty or imaginative, novel or compelling, but always rising from a tough reasonableness and often attaining startling insight, with moments of breathtaking beauty. In short, the conceit, with its wit and surprise and bias of reason, suited his mind, his many-sided interests and his poetic nature.[9]

The wit and the conceits are generously illustrated, but there is no venture beyond them by way of further analysis of poems. There is, however, frequent reference to the subject matter and recurrent themes of the poetry; this indicates that an examination may be made for determining to what extent the quality of a poem depends upon these, to what extent upon the technique, and upon the relation-

8

ship beween technique and subject matter. But these considerations are not kept distinct in Mr. Williamson's book. When he would appear to be talking about the technique of composition or the structure of a poem, he reiterates approvingly statements made by a poem. Upon Donne's "*Extasie*," a poem about the relationship of the bodies and souls of lovers, he offers this comment:

Here a Dionysian ecstasy is supported by the coolest reason, and neither feeling nor thought can be separated from its sensuous embodiment. This is no poetizing of thought, but thought in the flesh of sensuous and emotional perception, or mind expressing itself in the book of the body.[10]

An observation is made upon the conceit in somewhat the same manner:

We shall not be wrong if we conclude that the conceit is one of the principal means by which Donne chained analysis to ecstasy; never, we remember, more characteristically than in a poem called *The Extasie*.[11]

Mr. Williamson's book has a section especially devoted to a discussion of the conceit. Here he quotes definitions that have been made by others, and he agrees with the stress that is put upon certain aspects. These are the *discordia concors*, the intellectuality and the sincerity that obtain—in the words of T. E. Hulme—"when the whole of the analogy is necessary to get out the exact curve of the feeling or thing you want to express." [12] Here again, except for the *discordia concors*, which is another name for the conceit, general qualities are attributed and references are made to the author's mind: "sincerity" is particularly such a reference. Though he applies in detail the suggestions made by Mr. Eliot, Mr. Williamson makes no further advance in analysis of the poetry.

9

# JOHN CROWE RANSOM

In the writings of John Crowe Ransom we find a conception of metaphysical poetry which is categorial, beyond being historical. The term, as Mr. Ransom uses it, is evaluative, referring to a superior kind of poetry of which the seventeenth-century poets are the most successful practitioners. Although it is never explicitly stated, the theory that the poetry is characterized by an actually metaphysical content seems at first to be implied by some of Mr. Ransom's remarks. What, for instance, does he mean by miraculism?

"Metaphysics", or miraculism, informs a poetry which is the most original and exciting, and intellectually perhaps the most seasoned, that we know in our literature, and very probably it has few equivalents in other literatures. But it is evident that the metaphysical effects may be large-scale or they may be small-scale. (I believe that generically, or ontologically, no distinction is to be made between them.) If Donne and Cowley illustrate the small-scale effects, Milton will illustrate the large-scale ones, probably as a consequence of the fact that he wrote major poems.[13]

Unfortunately, though he does attend to specific poems for other purposes, Mr. Ransom never shows clearly how this *miraculism* is allied with a single poem. Such a demonstration would be most desirable, since he is clear enough about the technique of figurative language that results in the poetry he esteems most highly, and uses it as a measure for making critical judgments upon all poetry. In Mr. Ransom's opinion, there is a kind of knowledge—of the metaphysical aspects of human experience, as he might call it—which poetry alone can articulate. This opinion and his sweeping generic use of *metaphysical* are evident in the following quotation:

The intention of Metaphysical Poetry is to complement science, and improve discourse. Naturalistic discourse is incomplete for either of two reasons. It has the minimum of physical content and starves the sensibility, or it has the maximum, as if to avoid the appearance of evil, but is laborious and pointless. Platonic Poetry is too idealistic, but Physical Poetry is too realistic, and realism is tedious and does not maintain interest. The poets therefore introduce the psychological device of the miracle. The predication which it permits is clean and quick but it is not a scientific predication. For scientific predication concludes an act of attention but miraculism initiates one.[14]

One wishes that Mr. Ransom, so respectful to particulars, would point to a particular miracle. In poetry, before there can be a psychological device there must be a linguistic device. With such a device he does not fail to provide us, though when we would have him attend analytically to the device his utterance becomes psychological, and the transition from the device to the psychological seems yet to be explained. Mr. Ransom, like others, regards the conceit as this device:

For the critical mind Metaphysical Poetry refers perhaps almost entirely to the so-called "conceits" that constitute its staple. To define the conceit is to define small-scale Metaphysical Poetry.[15]

And in his definition of the conceit he again turns psychological (i.e., the terms of his statement make reference to impression, or feeling), although a certain use of the conceit is intimated:

A conceit originates in a metaphor; and in fact the conceit is but a metaphor if the metaphor is meant; that is, if it is developed so literally that it must be meant, or predicated so baldly that nothing else can be meant. Perhaps this will do for a definition.[16]

*Meant* is again one of those words that refer to a reader's final attitude toward a poem, but we cannot arrive at it by limiting discussion to terms that are an immediate reference to the poem. What Mr. Ransom is saying, obviously, is that the conceit is an extended comparison, a procession of statements that do not depart in figurativeness from a single metaphor. He says as much elsewhere:

I I

The impulse to metaphysical poetry, I shall assume, consists in committing the feelings in the case—those of unrequited love for example—to their determination within the elected figure.[17]

It is easily understood that such adherence to a figure may suggest that the figure is intended seriously or "meant". Yet Mr. Ransom surely would not contend "that nothing else can be meant". The figure is, after all, the mechanical device that represents or conveys what is meant—if one would bring up the difficult problem of meaning and the individual consciousness. What Mr. Ransom probably does intend is that the figure is not merely a mechanical intermediary, but an object with a peculiar individuality, and is to be contemplated as such. And one may add, as such to be studied and explained, for certain purposes. A distinction may be made between the structure of an object, and the quality of an object when related to human attention. There are times when one might wish that references to these in comment on poetry were less mixed, for the terminology of quality is always more variable—as distinguished from constant—than the terminology of structure. We find such a mixture when Mr. Ransom speaks of poetry that has

a single extended image to bear the whole weight of the conceptual structure, as is the way of that precision method of poetical composition which flourishes in the "metaphysical" style.[18]

The *extended image* is a detail of structure; *precision,* as Mr. Ransom uses it, is a quality attributed to the poetry. Extension of image is a method, but what it brings precision to, and why it does so, are left unexplained. That it does so pre-eminently for a concept is arguable, though it may suggest that a concept, with its qualitative accompaniments, is meant, is seriously intended.

A single extended metaphor constituting the whole poem is the primary definition in Mr. Ransom's conception of metaphysical poetry. This definition may be tested by looking for examples of it in the seventeenth century and by

studying that poetry to determine whether its "success"—
the dominant and most frequent structure of the poems—is
in the direction of the definition. At present it is interesting
to note the consistency of the highly restrictive definition
with Mr. Ransom's pronouncements on other, extraliterary
subjects. He has been much concerned, especially in his
earlier writings,[19] with religious myth, orthodoxy and ritual,
uttering a philosophy that held these things valuable and
found them wanting in modern society; our misfortune, he
argued, is that we have no single consistent myth which is
acceptably representative of life beyond its mere economic
and biological aspects and which provides adequately for
articulation of this life. When no single myth is meant,
ritual, which is a kind of articulation, becomes meaningless
or impossible. Mr. Ransom was not calling simply for a
religious creed:

Manners, rites, and arts are so close to each other that often
their occasions must be confused, and it does not matter much
if they are.[20]

The "occasion" for ritual generically includes the occasion
for writing a poem, and Mr. Ransom would have the poet
*mean* a single metaphor just as society should *mean* a single myth, which is a kind of cosmic metaphor that can be
extended to every peculiar detail of human experience.
Perhaps the critic should hesitate before Mr. Ransom's analogies. Possibly on linguistic-aesthetic-psychological grounds
he is right, but only possibly, by no means certainly. His
social philosophy, with its dicta and evaluations, merges so
continuously into his literary criticism that one wonders
whether an unprejudiced—a "scientific"—analysis of poetry
would fall neatly into the same locus or not.

The poem-ritual occasion is also connected with the term
*metaphysical* and Mr. Ransom's definition of it. It seems
that he uses *metaphysical* as if it were other than an acci-
dental term. Yet its meaning—e.g., miraculism—derives
more from his own psychologizing than from customary

13

philosophical usage; it refers to the sentiments and sensibilities of the individual:

The poet perpetuates in his poem an order of existence which in actual life is constantly crumbling beneath his touch.[21]

The result of Mr. Ransom's habit of bringing into synthesis his several opinions may be briefly indicated: metaphysical (seventeenth-century poetry→extended metaphor→order of existence); the terms in parentheses may be put in any order. Whether these references hang together by their own nature remains to be learned, although here we have taken note of such expressions as "order of existence" for learning the sources and implications of Mr. Ransom's definitions and need not retain them in a fresh analysis of poems.

## ALLEN TATE

We may expect that the criticism of Allen Tate will contain much of the same import to be found in that of Mr. Ransom, for each has announced his indebtedness to the other, and they have held similar attitudes on matters other than metaphysical poetry. We find indeed that this is true. Both critics hold metaphysical poetry in high esteem and see in it the same characteristics. One noticeable difference, however, is that Mr. Tate is less rigorous and positive in the technical lineaments that he attributes to the poetry. For him, as for Mr. Ransom, characterization of metaphysical poetry entails definition of the conceit. In this definition he concurs with Mr. Ransom, but he does not insist that the conceit of a metaphysical poem is necessarily or typically a metaphor so extended that it is coterminous with the whole structure of the poem (though he suggests that it may be so at times):

Therein lies the nature of the 'conceit'. It is an idea not inherent in the subject, but exactly parallel to it, elaborated beyond the usual stretch of metaphor into a supporting structure for a long passage or even an entire poem.[22]

When Mr. Tate treats of the matter at greater length his slight divergence from Mr. Ransom becomes clearer. Instead of committing himself to terminology such as *meantness* and such strict definiton as *a single extended metaphor*, he gives his statements the qualifications of approximateness, thus making for a looser category than that offered by Mr. Ransom. Mr. Tate sees in metaphysical poetry not "meantness", but an explicit logical order; not "a single extended image", but the characteristic development of imagery by logical extension. These correlatives to Mr. Ransom's terms are found in Mr. Tate's statement:

in metaphysical poetry the logical order is explicit; it must be coherent; the imagery by which it is sensuously embodied must have at least the look of logical determinism: I say the look of logic because the varieties of ambiguity and contradiction possible beneath the logical surface are endless . . . Here it is enough to say that the development of imagery by logical extension, the reasonable framework being an Ariadne's thread that the poet will not permit us to lose, is the hallmark of the poetry called metaphysical.[23]

We may restate this in other words: in metaphysical poetry there is conceptual development in imagistic terms, and the images can be recognized as connected with and following each other by their own nature, or else their relationship and sequence is explained within the poem. Such an account is fully applicable to poems, whether or not it would be found valid as a description when applied to Donne's. In testing this proposition one would not look for adherence to a single metaphor throughout a poem, but simply for a series of images that follow each other according to an intellective basis, this basis itself being suggested by the images.

Mr. Tate further characterizes metaphysical poetry by distinguishing it from poetry constituted by a series of images having no discernible intellective basis:

Strategy [metaphysical] would here indicate the point on the intensive-extensive scale at which the poet deploys his resources of meaning. The metaphysical poet as a rationalist begins at or near the extensive or denoting end of the line; the romantic or Symbolist poet at the other, intensive end; and each by a straining feat of the imagination tries to push his meanings as far as he can toward the opposite end, so as to occupy the entire scale.[24]

Mr. Tate's own language is not so near the denoting end of the line as one would have it. By "meanings" does he refer to distinguishable terms in poems that have been written, or does the word include the most ineffable intentions of a poet? Even if we could settle upon a definite reference for "meanings", we would still want a clear mechanical description of the process and product intimated by "a straining feat of the imagination." Whether or not it is reducible to actually descriptive definition, and whatever the terms of such definition might be, Mr. Tate does supply a general hypothesis: metaphysical and symbolist poetry are of similar linguistic materials (i.e., images), but these materials are organized in respective patterns that are technically the obverse of each other. Like the pronouncements of other critics, this hypothesis and Mr. Tate's definition of metaphysical poetry as "the development of imagery by logical extension" must be shown to rest upon analyses of particular poems.

## CLEANTH BROOKS

In his *Modern Poetry and the Tradition*, Cleanth Brooks treats at considerable length several problems concerning metaphysical poetry. He states in the preface that his book is in some measure the extension, application, and synthesis of ideas borrowed from other critics, including Eliot, Ransom, and Tate. Consequently, in discussing Mr. Brooks it is likely that there will be some repetition of material already reviewed.

It should first be noted that, to put it as simply as possible, Mr. Brooks regards metaphysical poetry as the best

16

kind of poetry—as, indeed, of the condition toward which any poem tends in so far as it is successful. Consequently, in characterizing the poetry, he is evaluative as well as descriptive. In his most elementary definition he is closer to Mr. Tate than to Mr. Ransom, for like Mr. Tate he refrains from insisting upon the single extended metaphor as normally the framework of a metaphysical poem, although he does of course identify metaphorical device with the body of the poem:

Most clearly of all, the metaphysical poets reveal the essentially functional character of all metaphor. We cannot remove the comparisons from their poems, as we might remove ornaments and illustrations attached to a statement, without demolishing the poem. The comparison *is* the poem in a structural sense.[25]

This, like similar statements previously observed, suggests the question: Is a typical poem by Donne and his fellow poets based on a conceit or unbroken chain of conceits, or can we say only that it is a poem in which the conceit appears frequently?

In further development of the subject Mr. Brooks suggests that he considers *metaphysical* as an arbitrary name, that it designates a poetry the definition of which is partially fulfilled by other poetry in more or less measure. Moreover, with the definition he has already given, he identifies the term *wit*:

One might, indeed, let the matter rest on the definition of wit: viz., metaphysical poetry (whatever the term metaphysical may mean or may have meant) is witty poetry. . . . Our definition of metaphysical poetry, then, will have to treat the difference between metaphysical poetry, and other poetry as a difference of degree, not of kind.[26]

Mr. Brooks has singled out what he considers to be the essential feature of metaphysical poetry and applied it to other poetry; and obviously this process gives hierarchical advantage to the metaphysical. Whether this is demon-

17

strable and just, remains problematical. What is to prevent the advocate of another poetry from laying down as the rule what he considers essentially poetical, even if Mr. Brooks is altogether accurate in his description of metaphysical poetry?

With the identification of the definitions of metaphysical poetry and wit Mr. Brooks goes beyond what is primarily structural description. This would not be the case if he meant simply that statement made by metaphor and imagery is fundamentally the device of wit, as he uses that term. But he makes clear that by wit he means not structure alone:

> Wit is not merely an acute perception of analogies; it is a lively awareness of the fact that the obvious attitude toward a given situation is not the only possible attitude.[27]

This awareness must be ascribed to the poet; though it is deduced from the poetry, it does not inhere in the poetic technique and consequently is not pertinent to technical distinctions, which are those first insisted upon by Mr. Brooks and other critics. If we are to accept the first definition as distinguishing the poetry we must see how the generalizations departing from the terminology of structure are consequent upon this definition.

Mr. Brooks' contribution in emphasizing the wittiness of metaphysical poetry is to suggest that this poetry is characterized not only by the manner of its statement but also by the import of its statement (i.e., the thought ultimately represented by the words of a passage or poem). He denominates the metaphysical poet as witty because of the poet's use of metaphor and because "he converges his lines from the farthest possible distances" [28]—the *discordia concors* again; and the same wit he credits for the irony and complexity of attitudes to be observed in the statement of the poem. The connection between the structure and the kind of statement is left in question. Does the nature of the statement follow causally from the structure, or are such statement and structure in combination merely coincidental in the poetry of the seventeenth century? This question may in some measure be settled by attending to the poetry; we may determine whether the wit of a passage is felt because of the technique used or because of the thought contained; and if the force of the passage is found to arise from the thought, then we should want to know what is contributed by the technique and what is the relationship between technique and thought in so far as the force or effect of wit is concerned.

Mr. Brooks presents another problem, one we have already met in the comment of Mr. Tate. He suggests that metaphysical poetry and symbolist poetry share essentially characteristic features. In doing so he indicates further the qualified emphasis he gives to the structural aspect of metaphysical poetry. Instead of placing symbolist poetry in positive structural relation to metaphysical, he seems to belittle the importance of structure with regard to all poetry:

Lack of dependence on logical structure distinguishes symbolist poetry from simple expository prose; but this is also true of poetry in general.[29]

The strategy, or technique, of metaphysical poetry, which he and other critics have considered so seriously, diminishes in importance when he relates this poetry to another kind:

There are various strategies which the poet may employ, but we shall only confuse matters if we try to make more than a distinction of strategy between the characteristic methods of the metaphysical poet and the symbolist poet.[30]

A more rigid formulator of structural pattern for metaphysical poetry, Mr. Ransom has not failed to take issue with Mr. Brooks on this score:

But I think that the matter of the logic might have engaged him a little more deeply. In view of the logical showing of the seventeenth century he might have argued that the old poets were wasting some of their labors, for the logical nicety is much the most visible of their superficial techniques, and goes far beyond what Mr. Brooks cares to require.[31]

However this issue may eventually be settled, it is apparent that Mr. Brooks presents a new point of view on metaphysical poetry. For him, definition of its structure in technical terms is insufficient characterization of the poetry. He eventually forsakes explanation that is objectively determinable in the structure of the poetry, and he arrives at a description of the poetry by laying stress rather upon its pervasive features and communicative service to the poet than upon its pattern of organization:

With the acquisition of these qualities—irony, realistic diction, wit—symbolist poetry coalesces with metaphysical.[32]

There was in Donne's poetry an ambiguity which went far deeper than the mere use of obscure and difficult references. There was—as there is in the case of tragedy—an ambiguity as to the poet's ultimate attitude.[33]

The account of the subject which Mr. Brooks presents is not wholly consistent; he fails to indicate the development from the structure of a poetry to the "poet's ultimate attitude". But it is likely that his complicating of problems and difficulties does a kind of justice to the subject.

## SUMMARY

We may now bring together those remarks, singled out from comment on metaphysical poetry, which actually can be referred to the poetry itself. Our critics agree in the generalization that the poetry is characterized by the conceit and by wit. The conceit is regarded as a comparison of the dissimilar, frequently an extended comparison. As to the exact relationship of the conceit to metaphysical poetry, there is no final and common explanation among the critics. The several statements on the subject are, in effect, as follows:

The conceit is simply a frequent, a habitual device in the poetry.

The conceit, as it is distinctive of an exemplary metaphysical poem, is a single extended metaphor comprising the whole poem.

The metaphysical poem, not necessarily based on a single metaphor, at no point departs from the manner of the conceit, the poem showing a development of imagery by logical extension.

Whatever thought may be extracted or restated from a typical passage of metaphysical poetry is, in the passage, expressed by a trope.

As a characterization, wit, of course, remains more general than conceit. If the poetry is to be distinguished by structural device alone, one may mean simply that the conceit is a device of wit. One can also mean that there are in metaphysical poetry the conceit and other wit devices comparable to it, though such devices have not been specified by any critic. One critic, regarding metaphysical poetry as witty, departs from a rigidly structural aspect and sees wit as a pervasive quality of the poetry. A more specific observation from this point of view is to the effect that metaphysical poetry is witty by its expression of irony and complexity of attitude.

# Chapter II

## THE POEMS

### Donne's *Songs and Sonets*

JOHN DONNE is considered the most prominent of the group of seventeenth-century poets called metaphysical, and statements on metaphysical poetry most often refer to the poems of his *Songs and Sonets*. It is, therefore, natural that further study of the subject should attend to these. (The text consistently used here is *The Poems of John Donne*, ed. Sir H. J. C. Grierson. London, Oxford, 1933.)

### THE GOOD MORROW

The opening lines and title of "The Good Morrow", as well as other parts of the poem, indicate that it is addressed by a lover to his loved one after a night of love. Speculation on what the lovers did until they loved is in the form of a conceit; the lovers are equated with suckling children:

> . . . were we not wean'd till then?
> But suck'd on countrey pleasures, childishly?

The poem does not develop by an extension of this conceit nor are references to infancy or the stages of human growth made again as statements upon the condition of the lovers, past or present. Instead, the conceit is followed by an alter-

native conceit; previous to this love the lovers were as in-
fants, or their unawareness was a condition of sleeping in
the legendary den of the seven sleepers. So the speculation
runs. But there is hardly a development of thought in the
sequence of these two conceits, and there is no linkage between them in figurative terms. And since the two conceits
are independent of each other and yet reiterative in statement, their possibilities of precision and significance of
detail become less likely when it is affirmed concerning both
of them that "T'was so." First the conceits are on a par
with each other and then they are lumped together, so that
what issues from them is a general implication, not a conceptual argument developed by a single figure or even a
series of figures. In the closing lines of the stanza the
speaker turns from the pre-love condition to the present:
except for his love, he says, all pleasures are fancies, and
all his former experience of beauty was but a dream of the
loved one. These statements, although suggestive of conceits, are hardly more than the idioms of hyperbole. They
do not continue previous references in the poem, nor are
they recalled in later references.

As the lover's speech continues in the second stanza
there is no continuation of either argument or terminology
from the first stanza. It is not until the fourth line that the
figurative language of a conceit occurs. Following the generalization,

> For love, all love of other sights controules,

there comes the particular example,

> And makes one little roome, an every where.

The conceit is constituted by the identification of a room
with the world. Other geographical references follow this
conceit, but the conceit itself is not in any way extended.
The lines that follow,

> Let sea-discoverers to new worlds have gone,
> Let Maps to other, worlds on worlds have showne,

23

are rhetorical imperatives exclaimed by the lover in expression of his indifference to and independence of affairs other than his own. There is nothing figurative in these statements. Their terminology, however, serves as a referential background for the conceit used in the final line of the stanza:

Let us possesse one world, each hath one, and is one.

This time each of the lovers is identified with a world. To call this trope a conceit is perhaps questionable, unless one means by a conceit any metaphor or other figure that is not utterly conventional.

The third stanza opens with literal description: the lovers' faces are reflected in each other's eyes. The second line, "And true plain hearts doe in the faces rest," is hardly less literal, since the word *heart* is considered synonymous with *affections* rather than figuratively representative of *affections*. In the next two lines we do have a conceit:

Where can we finde two better hemispheares
Without sharpe North, without declining West?

This is not the first use of geographical terms. Previously it was said that each lover was a world, that each possessed a world. However calculated and noticeable the use of two "geographical" conceits may be, one is in no way the logical extension or justification of the other. The conceits stand independently side by side; one does not continue from the other. A connection between them is suggested by the fact that each makes reference to the same material, but the connection is general, even vague. Moreover, the second conceit, though it develops its own meaning, does not add meaning to the first. The second conceit says that the faces in which hearts rest are hemispheres, but of a kind that presents no perils to mariners. The implication is that the lovers have nothing to fear from each other and may be confident about the course of their love. The poem ends with a new conceit:

What ever dyes, was not mixt equally;
If our two loves be one, or, thou and I
Love so alike, that none doe slacken, none can die.

Here the conceit is constituted by the application of a proposition from physical science to the relationship of the
lovers. If their love is a single unity or is made of equal
parts, then, like similar mixtures, the relationship will hold
fast and neither party will cease loving the other. The idea
of equal parts may refer to the hemispheres of the earlier
conceit, but the connection between the two conceits is so
slight it can hardly be considered that one is the extension
of the other. If one attempts to include the hemispheres in
the conceit of the mixture, it becomes apparent that no
meaningful resolution is possible, although the final conceit is otherwise a development in the meaning of the poem.

This examination of "The Good Morrow" is not an attempt at evaluating the poem. Our concern is to discover
which statements about the structure of metaphysical poetry are borne out by it. The only statement that is found
to be wholly valid with regard to "The Good Morrow" is
that the conceit often occurs. It can also be said that the
ideological burden of the poem is to a considerable extent
conveyed by the use of tropes, though not consistently. An
obvious, or superficial, wit inheres in the conceits and such
devices as the hyperbole of the first stanza and the rhetorical
imperatives of the second. Another kind of wit, less local
and rhetorical, may be considered as present in the poem.
This wit consists in the contrast between the two *worlds*:
the world of the lovers, and the geographical world. It is,
moreover, not merely a verbal wit, for each world represents
an attitude—the worldly attitude and the lover's attitude.
There is, then, a complexity of attitudes in the poem. But
the lover, who speaks the poem, gives no hint of being
involved in an ironical situation, of entertaining any complexity of attitudes. He dismisses the geographical world
and affirms the world of love.

# THE CANONIZATION

The first stanza of "The Canonization" constitutes an apostrophe to anyone who might try to distract or persuade the lover from his loving. The lover, implying that he is determined upon loving, suggests that his critic admonish him upon other grounds, or that the critic attend to his own advancement, but at any rate leave the lover undisturbed. Aside from the apostrophe, there is no figurativeness in this stanza, and there is no development or addition of statement after the first line. A wittiness results from grouping together the several specific actions, each of which might be performed as alternatives to criticizing the lover; from the critic's point of view it is irrelevant and absurd to consider such alternatives. Though the stanza is from one point of view repetitious, though it contains no trope or material that is to be figuratively elaborated, its wit does characterize the speaker and establish a tone.

This tone is maintained with little change throughout the second stanza, which is similar to the first in its construction and scarcely different in its statement. The speaker continues the argument for his love, this time in the manner of rhetorical interrogations. He asks what injuries may be charged against his loving, and then, in the form of questions, lists specific possibilities: have his sighs drowned ships? have his tears flooded grounds? have his lover's-chills affected the weather? have his lover's-fevers affected the health of society? These possibilities, by the extent of their exaggeration, border upon metaphor, but the obvious function of the exaggeration is the absurdity which makes for wit. An additional element in the wit is the fact that the issues raised by the lover are irrelevant to—are a digression from—sensible arguments which might be brought against him. The same kind of wit is produced by the literal statement of the lines concluding the stanza:

> Soldiers finde warres, and Lawyers finde out still
> Litigious men, which quarrels move,
> Though she and I do love.

26

This observation, though it may be witty by its absurdity in the apparent argument, is on another level of reading not absurd at all, though still witty. With these final lines of the second stanza it becomes obvious that the lover is doing more than making a witty appeal for permission to continue his loving undisturbed. He is saying that his loving has no effect upon soldiers, lawyers and litigious men; and he is implying, here and throughout the preceding part of the poem, that the values of the lover and those of the world are wholly different and unconnected. In the first two stanzas the speaker has illustrated the thesis that it is absurd to make worldly values bear upon the lover. His absurd defiance of the world is, indirectly, the suggestion of a serious defiance, and this practice of indirection is witty. It should be noticed that this wit does not depend upon the particular devices used for overt absurdity. Like the wit of "The Good Morrow", it proceeds from the contrast of the two attitudes: that of the world, and that of the lover. Here, however, the lover does not easily dismiss the world. He is cognizant of the contrasting attitudes as being in conflict, and he is opposing one to the other. He is insisting upon a complexity of attitudes, arguing that one attitude should not be confused with or subordinated to the other. Throughout the rest of the poem he continues to argue for the merit and self-sufficiency of the lover's world, the lover's attitude.

The third stanza begins with the lover's statement of his indifference to what others think of or call the lovers. And the stanza continues with the lover's own suggestions as to how they may be characterized: they are tapers, dying at their own cost; in them may be found the Eagle and the Dove; finally, they are comparable to the riddle of the Phœnix:

> The Phœnix ridle hath more wit
> By us, we two being one, are it.
> So to one neutrall thing both sexes fit,
> Wee dye and rise the same, and prove
> Mysterious by this love.

These comparisons, particularly the latter, may be regarded as conceits. There is, however, no connection between the conceits in so far as their terms are concerned; but each one does make the witty point of the paradoxical—the mysterious—nature of the lovers' relationship.

None of the earlier conceits is drawn upon in the fourth stanza, which begins with the statement that the lovers can die by love, a possibility suggested in the preceding stanza. The statement is without metaphor and says in effect that when the lovers have died, their legend may not be fit for tombs and hearse, but it will be fit for verse. In the lines that follow, the subject is further developed, this time with an abundant use of metaphor:

> And if no peece of Chronicle wee prove,
> We'll build in sonnets pretty roomes;
> As well a well wrought urne becomes
> The greatest ashes, as halfe-acre tombes,
> And by these hymnes, all shall approve
> Us *Canoniz'd* for Love:

Though there are several metaphors here, the passage is not constituted by a single conceit; we do not have logical extension in the terms of an initial image or other metaphorical situation. There is, however, no lapse of metaphorical statement. The conceits follow immediately upon each other and are joined to each other by obvious association. One example of such association is the shift from *verse* to *sonnets* to *hymns*. Another example: the sonnets containing the story of the lovers are like pretty rooms in which the lovers themselves are contained; the sonnets—or pretty rooms—are like a well wrought urn, as distinguished from some monument of greater proportions. And finally, having shifted from sonnets to hymns, the passage ends with the statement that the lovers are canonized. This conclusion is reached by no argument, it is not contained within a metaphorical development: as we have already observed, it proceeds simply by an obvious association.

The conceit of canonization continues throughout the final stanza of the poem. This continuation of the conceit may be regarded as a single segment of extension, for the extension is effected by a statement, comprising the whole stanza, which invokes the lovers as canonized—as saints:

> And thus invoke us; You whom reverend love
> Made one anothers hermitage;
> You, to whom love was peace, that now is rage;
> Who did the whole worlds soule contract, and drove
> Into the glasses of your eyes
> So made such mirrors, and such spies,
> That they did all to you epitomize,
> Countries, Townes, Courts: Beg from above
> A patterne of your love!

The elements contained in this stanza are themselves tropes proper to the religious invocation which is the embracing conceit: the lovers had a hermitage—one another—in which they found peace and performed the miracle of contracting the world. The stanza ends with a request to the lovers that they "beg from above" a pattern of their love, which is their special function as saints.

We may turn now to observation of the general structure of the poem in its entirety. It may be said of the last three stanzas of "The Canonization" that the conceit is frequent. A negative argument could be made, however, on the basis that there are no conceits in the first two stanzas. At any rate, even if the issue of frequency could be settled in the affirmative, this affirmation would contribute little of importance to the more complicated and systematic definitions of metaphysical poetry which several critics have ventured.

Our analysis has shown that "The Canonization" is not built on a single extended metaphor that is coterminous with the poem. One could argue that the embracing metaphor is constituted by the situation out of which the poem is supposedly uttered—the lover in defense of his loving—and that the poem has implications beyond its obvious verbal reference; but then such argument must make allowance for dramatic monologues and poems with other kinds of unity to be included under *metaphysical*, and as a result the term and its definition become meaningless and unprofitable. It is true that the conceit that gives the poem its title has considerable extension, but it is unanticipated and unpredictable until reached in the poem; the extent of the conceit is too slight in relation to the rest of the poem to justify its being regarded as characterizing the general structure of the entire poem.

According to our analysis of the first two stanzas, one cannot say of "The Canonization" that it departs at no point from the manner of the conceit, or that a prose restatement of the poem's meaning is within the poem always expressed by a trope. There are, however, passages in the poem made up wholly of conceit following upon conceit, and often it is a conceit or sequence of conceits which expresses whatever thought may be inferred or restated from the poetry. Our analysis confirms that "The Canonization" is witty in that it contains the devices of wit: the absurd apostrophes of the first stanza, the exaggerations and rhetorical questions of the second, and the associations and conceits in the remaining stanza. We observed, moreover, that there is in the poem wit which results from a complexity of attitudes, which is conceptual originally, and which does not follow from local rhetorical device.

## TWICKNAM GARDEN

Donne's "Twicknam Garden" is, in its title and structure, unlike many of his other poems. For instance, poems having some figurative use of titles within the poetry are "The Sunne Rising", "The Flea", "The Will", and other poems, and even "A Nocturnall upon Saint Lucies Day", which is peculiarly similar to "Twicknam Garden" in several respects. Unless we seek in the biography of the poet for additional meanings, the title of this poem is to be taken simply and literally: the speaker of the poem is present in the garden and makes references to its details.

The garden, then, may be regarded as an immediate material of the poem. Another immediate material would be the speaker's feelings, his emotional condition. These two materials are introduced and developed side by side: the poem begins

> Blasted with sighs, and surrounded with teares,
> Hither I come to seeke the spring, . . .

And not until the end of the poem does the speaker pursue any argument or set up any extended metaphor as a seeming fulfillment to the direction of the whole poem. He continues speaking in the terms with which the poem begins, and the terms are actually what the poem is about—the garden and his emotion. The speaker actually discusses the relationship between these; he refers to the garden as it is seen in the light of the emotion and, thus seen, as it reflects the emotion. We have, consequently, an essentially dramatic poem: a speaker in a specific situation making utterances about the situation:

> Blasted with sighs, and surrounded with teares,
> Hither I come to seeke the spring,
> And at mine eyes, and at mine eares,
> Receive such balmes, as else cure every thing;
> But O, selfe traytor, I do bring
> The spider love, which transubstantiates all,
> And can convert Manna to gall,
> And that this place may thoroughly be thought
> True Paradise, I have the serpent brought.

Although the dramatic situation of the speaker is to be taken literally, his utterance does none the less contain figurative expressions. The speaker, given over to sighs and tears, comes to the garden at the spring season, seeking some relief. The garden, with its pleasant aspects of sight and sound, would work a healing effect upon him but for the fact that he has brought the "spider love." Here we have the first conceit of the poem. This conceit—love as a spider—is extended, but with the extension the metaphor changes its terms. The emotion of love, like the spider, corrupts the pleasures of the garden. And, like religious love, it "transubstantiates" these, only with an ironical difference; for instead of providing healthy spiritual nourishment, this love changes a provident remedy—manna—into unpalatable bitterness. The speaker leaves this complex figure and continues his irony, saying that he has brought along the serpent in order that this garden may be considered a true paradise, for the traditional paradise—the Garden of Eden —had a serpent in it. This statement is far more complicated dramatically than it is rhetorically. It is in sheer irony that the speaker says he has brought the serpent purposefully. Though with the addition of the serpent the garden is made comparable to the traditional paradise, no paradisaical benefits are implied: one garden is like the other because both are invaded by evil. We see, thus, that the *serpent* is related to the general logic of its context: it is conveyed by the speaker to the garden, and this is said as part of a consistent comment upon the garden.

But how, in the first place, is the presence of the serpent to be explained? Certainly it is not to be pictured as part of a physical setting suggested by the poem. (Of course, it is there in the garden, but not in a physical sense, not as an image.) Obviously, the serpent represents that emotion of the speaker which makes it impossible for him to appreciate the pleasures of the garden, which turns these to displeasures. (One may be reminded of "a serpent in the breast".) This equation between serpent and emotion is, however, not stated. We have, consequently, an implied metaphor: a symbol is used in the place of the thing symbolized while there is no grammatical connection between the two—the thing symbolized, in fact, being omitted. An effect of the poetry is this suggestion of the nature of the emotion: we may have here something comparable to the technique of symbolist poetry. The emotion is the *subject* of the poem, and the speaker, in order to specify its character, must go beyond the statement that all is not well with him; to characterize the emotion he must discuss it in terms other than itself. And such terms are the peculiar aspect of the garden, the spider, and the serpent. All these are meaningful in that they suggest characterizations of the emotion. It is, I believe, terms such as these that would be important in a consideration of poetic effect. A symbolist poem of comparable terms would be "difficult" in so far as one could not determine the *subject* of which the terms are characterizations, the theme by which they cohere.

In the second stanza of the poem the speaker continues referring to his emotion by elaborating upon the fact that he is unable to appreciate the pleasant garden; a dismal garden would be more tolerable to his mood:

> 'Twere wholsomer for mee, that winter did
>  Benight the glory of this place,
>  And that a grave frost did forbid
> These trees to laugh, and mocke mee to my face;
>  But that I may not this disgrace
> Indure, nor yet leave loving, Love let mee
>  Some senslesse peece of this place bee;
> Make me a mandrake, so I may groane here,
>  Or a stone fountaine weeping out my yeare.

Here again it is apparent that the passage is not constituted by conceit—one or more. There is, of course, some figurativeness, but the meaning or effect of the passage depends upon its dramatic significance, figurative or not. Everything the speaker says, like the mention of the serpent in the first stanza, serves to intimate the quality of his emotion. The stanza begins with a conditional statement: a winter garden would be more tolerable and fitting to his feelings than a spring garden; in such a garden the trees would not laugh and mock him to his face, as they do now. The laughing, mocking trees are a metaphor (or personification), but this

33

metaphor does not determine or extend the structure of the poem. And it is no criticism of the passage to say this. The trees become terms in a figurative expression because they are part of a situation that the speaker observes to be ironical. Here the figurativeness is dramatic rather than structural, as we have been using that word. It is dramatically significant that the speaker should make the figure, and the intimation already noted continues. It does, indeed, continue through the entire stanza. The spring garden remains unchanged, of course, so the speaker requests of "Love" (obviously the deity) that, in order not to endure "this disgrace" of mockery and yet to cease not from loving, he be made a "senseless peece" of the garden—a groaning mandrake (of folklore) or a weeping stone fountain. There is no logic and certainly no feasibility to the request. How, as a senseless object, though "groaning" or "weeping", would he continue to love? The question is a confusing one if we try to follow it literally and rationally. But this is beside the point. Because it is thus confusing, the more obviously is the question, again like other parts of the poem, connotatively an intimation of the speaker's emotion. And here, too, we may notice, there is some figurativeness, but it is incidental in the passage and subordinate to it. This is not to say that it is a detachable ornament; it is an element of the intimating rhetorical question that we have discussed.

In this second stanza there is some development of the subject of the poem, and this advance is contained in the phrase "nor yet leave loving." Such characterization of the emotion, which has been called "spider" and "serpent", suggests its tension and complexity. It should be noticed, however, that in the poem as we have read it thus far there has been no development of idea through argument or extended metaphors (cf. "A Valediction: Forbidding Mourning", "The Extasie", "A Lecture upon the Shadow") but rather a developmental reference to the emotion which is the subject of the poem.

The opening of the third and final stanza is, in a way,

34

comparable to extended metaphor, and the whole stanza differs, by its argumentative nature, from the first two.

> Hither with christall vyals, lovers come,
>     And take my teares, which are loves wine,
>     And try your mistresse Teares at home,
> For all are false, that tast not just like mine;
>     Alas, hearts do not in eyes shine,
> Nor can you more judge womans thoughts by teares,
> Then by her shadow, what she weares.
> O perverse sexe, where none is true but shee,
>     Who's therefore true, because her truth kills mee.

The metaphor extended is that of the speaker as a weeping stone fountain, this having been suggested at the end of the preceding stanza. Extension of this metaphor, however, does not consist in elaboration but rather in maintained reference to the initial metaphorical situation. The speaker bids lovers to come with vials and take the tears which he, as fountain, is weeping. He calls the tears "loves wine", thus implying that they are a liquid accompaniment to the occasion of love and that they belong to a class within which distinctions may be made, as the connoisseur distinguishes among wines. The lovers are to compare these tears with those of their mistresses in order to discover the genuineness of the latter: "For all are false, that tast not just like mine." Thus the speaker exclaims upon the genuineness and seriousness of his own emotion; and at the same time suggests the source and experiential context of the emotion. That he has been personally affected by the nature of woman is emphasized by the "Alas" which introduces his dictum: woman's heart and thought are no more to be learned from her eyes and tears than is what she wears from her shadow. In other words, women are dissemblers, making for inconsistency, illogicality and disorder. They are a "perverse sexe", for, in the experience of the speaker, one of them by being true causes him to suffer. Her trueness consists in that she does not love him and

35

gives him this plainly to understand. Hence in a perverse and ironical sense of true, she is true in her attitude of not being his true love.

If we look back now over the stanza we find in it several metaphors: the speaker as fountain, tears as wine, the taste of tears as an indication of sincerity, and eyes as reflecting the heart. No one of these metaphors, however, includes all the others or provides the terms which are used in an expression of the central thought or subject of the poem. And though the metaphors are close upon each other, there is no logical extension of imagery. For example, the lovers' tasting the tears of their mistresses is not important as an image. If we want to make a comparable description for the development of the stanza, we might call it an associational procession of ideas. The concluding passage of the stanza ("O perverse sexe . . .") contains no metaphor ("her truth kills me" is hardly considerable for its figurativeness); nor can the passage be figuratively connected with any preceding metaphor.

It was observed above that the final stanza differs somewhat from the others. These stanzas, we noticed, made no argument, developed no idea, but as a dramatic utterance made reference to the garden and the emotion of the speaker, thus apparently characterizing the emotion. But in the final stanza there is argument and development of idea: women are generally false, and one woman's "truth" is peculiar in that it affects the speaker painfully. These ideas offer themselves for consideration as ideas, and because of this the stanza is not so apparently a characterization of the speaker's emotion, which in the earlier stanzas is unmistakably the subject. Such observation may be in the nature of a criticism. There is a possible reading of the last stanza, and I believe it to be not unjust, which would make this criticism less strictly applicable. This reading would take the stanza as a dramatic utterance comparable to the others, despite the obtrusivenes of its ideas. That is, it would be found significant beyond its specific structure and immediate references, significant primarily in its reference to and characterization of the speaker's emotion.

## OTHER POEMS

We have found that no single characterization of metaphysical poetry is wholly borne out by any of the three poems we have examined. It is true that there are some conceits in each of these, and it may therefore be said that the conceit often occurs; but, as we have observed before, this is unpretentious beside the other definitions and would probably be found acceptable by proponents of these definitions. Consequently, it will not alter our problem or our approach to the problem if these three poems are, in their content of conceits, a fair sample of the rest of Donne's *Songs and Sonets*. These other poems we shall not examine in full detail, since the three analyses already made will provide a basis of reference and allow of some economy.

It will be convenient to continue the discussion of Donne's poems by allying them with the conclusions drawn from those already analyzed; it should be noted, however, that the three poems are not offered as representing a possible grouping of Donne's poems. To begin with "The Good Morrow": it was found that none of the definitions wholly fits. To some extent the ideological burden of the poem is conveyed by the use of tropes (metaphor-conceits and other tropes) but not in sufficient measure to justify this practice as characterizing the whole structure of the poem. Like "The Good Morrow", the poem beginning "Goe, and catche a falling starre" is conspicuously not an example of any of the definitions. We may say that it contains no conceits at all, unless it would be argued that any metaphor is a conceit. There are three, and only three, metaphors in the poem: these are

> Or to keep off envies stinging, . . .
> Till age snow white haires on thee, . . .
> Such a Pilgrimage were sweet; . . .

37

And these metaphors are obviously idiomatic (except for "Pilgrimage", perhaps) rather than of figurative force. Most of the images of the poem are contained in fanciful imperatives like the opening line. These imperatives are clearly impossible and hence are techniques of wit. The "prose meaning" of the poem is that there are no women both true and fair, under any circumstances, not anywhere in the world. This is said ironically—by devices of wit—in the first two stanzas, and it is said simply, without irony, in the last stanza. The poem, however, will not serve to illustrate the non-structural definition; it contains ironical technique but is not itself the expression of an irony, or complexity of attitude, its attitude (no true, fair women) being uncomplicated and steadily maintained.

Though there are differences among them, neither "The Sunne Rising", "The Indifferent", nor "Confined Love" provides a basis for the definitions. "The Sunne Rising" is the most richly figurative of the three poems. Like "The Good Morrow", it is the utterance of a lover after a night of love. (A picture of the lovers in a bedroom is suggested.) The whole poem is an apostrophe to the sun, giving it a surprising and somewhat funny personification. In addressing the sun, questioning and commanding it, the speaker says in effect that love is indifferent to all the influences that the sun has upon the world. He is thus in a position like that of the speaker of "The Good Morrow". He does not maintain or arrive at a complexity of attitudes, but he chooses one attitude from a complexity—that of love, and dismisses the other—the attitude of the world. This is said finally, at the end of the first stanza, with directness:

> Love, all alike, no season knowes, nor clyme,
> Nor houres, dayes, moneths, which are the rags of time.

The speaker continues to the effect that his love is complete in itself, as if it included everything in the world, everything under the sun. This is said in a conceit, the conceit being established at the end of the second stanza and extended through the third stanza, which is the final one. These lines, occurring within the conceit, will indicate the use of the metaphor:

> Thine age askes ease, and since thy duties bee
> To warme the world, that's done in warming us.

Though the conceit makes up a fairly long passage, there is no ideological development in it; it says throughout that the lovers are in themselves as complete as the world, thus, by implication, contrasting two "worlds" of value.

"The Indifferent" is much simpler rhetorically than "The Sunne Rising". It has no large measure of figurativeness, few conceits—and these of brief extent. Like almost every poem of Donne's, it is the statement of a speaker. Here the speaker expresses an unconventional and unromantic attitude toward love. He is inconstant, unfaithful, indiscriminate, promiscuous, and he says that all men and women should be so. There are local ironies in the poem, such as

> Or doth a feare, that men are true, torment you?

but the speaker's attitude, the attitude of the poem, remains single and unchanged. These same conclusions will serve for "Confined Love". Its thesis is that a woman should not be bound in love only to one man. This is expressed by implied analogies, such as: "Who e'r rigg'd faire ship to lie in harbors"; and it is stated literally and generally at the end of the poem:

> Good is not good, unlesse
> A thousand it possesse,
> But doth wast with greedinesse.

Poems having a similar relation to the definitions we have in mind are "Break of Day", "The Message", "The Curse", and others.

39

# THE PROHIBITION

"The Prohibition" is characteristic of Donne in its argument and paradox, but none of the definitions according to conceit is applicable to it. The poem is one of counsel addressed by a lover to a woman. It is composed of three stanzas, each with its own thesis: 1) Take heed of loving me; 2) Take heed of hating me; 3) Love and hate me, too. There are no conceits in the first stanza. Here the lover cautions heed in loving him, and he explains the need of caution, thus implying the nature of the former relation between himself and the woman. There is no danger that he, when loved, will be as she was when he loved her:

> By being to thee then what to me thou wast; . . .

The danger is that the joy of being loved may kill him, thus leaving her love frustrated:

> Then, least thy love, by my death, frustrate bee,
> If thou love mee, take heed of loving mee.

In the second stanza he warns her against hating him or taking "too much triumph in the Victorie." Her fear should be, not that he will retaliate, but that, destroying him by her hate, she will be deprived of her conquest. All this is expressed in military terms as a conceit, though the conceit does not extend beyond this stanza. In the final stanza the lover's argument develops into paradox: he would be both loved and hated:

> Love mee, that I may die the gentler way;
> Hate mee, because thy love'is too great for mee; . . .

When both attitudes are maintained, they counterbalance each other and he survives, escaping the sudden and violent death which love or hate singly would effect. (In Donne's time "die the gentler way" must certainly have been a pun, since *die* was also a verb for the sexual act.) His survival is stated as profitable for the woman, for thus he remains her field of activity and she may continue to love and hate:

> So shall I, live, thy Stage, not triumph bee; . . .

"Stage" and "Triumph" are the only conceits—if they can be so called—in the stanza. The conceit of the second stanza is of slight figurative force, for most of the figurative terms there are what they would be ordinarily; if it were not for the presence of *officer* such terms as *triumph, Victorie, retaliate, conquest* and *perish* would not necessarily have metaphorical status. We find, then, that the structure and effect of "The Prohibition" would not be wholly lost in a prose paraphrase that eliminated all figurativeness. In other words, the structure is not dependent upon tropes, but upon the sequence of ideas and combination of ideas. A complexity of attitude is here the explicit, rather than implicit, subject of the poem. Not only is the speaker's attitude complex, but so is that of the one spoken to, and therefore the situation involving them is a pattern of complex attitudes. All this is immediately in the poem.


## COMMUNITIE

Another argumentative poem of Donne's is "Communitie". The poem is about *good* and *bad,* the nature of women, and men's use of them. Its first three stanzas are speculative generalization meager in imagery and figurativeness. The first stanza is most general of all, wholly in terms of abstractions:

> Good wee must love, and must hate ill,
>     For ill is ill, and good good still,
>         But there are things indifferent,
>     Which wee may neither hate, nor love,
>     But one, and then another prove,
>         As wee shall finde our fancy bent.

The rest of the poem is an application of this thesis. It is

41

assumed in the second stanza that women are "things indifferent," and consequently are subject to the usage such things receive. In the second stanza this character of women —that they are neither good nor bad—is "proved" by false, question-begging statements, such as "Good is as visible as greene." And again the thesis is applied: "they deserve nor blame, nor praise." That is, they are not subject to moral judgment. And the argument is repeated and particularized, in violation of logic, with the development of a conceit that makes up the fourth and final stanza. Women are like fruit in the respect that they are not subject to moral judgment. It then follows, illogically as if logically, that they are like fruit in other respects: they may be used, as a mere commodity, without the raising of moral issue; the poem ends—

> And when hee hath the kernell eate,
> Who doth not fling away the shell?

There is in "Communitie" witty argument, not achieved through paradox (which is overtly an apparent contradiction of logic), but through discourse that moves with the assurance of logic and yet is obviously fallacious. The wit consists in ingenuity, in the semblance of logical support upon which an attitude is rested. As we have observed, the poem develops by proceeding from the general to the particular, ending finally with the only conceit of the poem and thus arriving at the attitude which is the destination of the argument. The attitude is not witty in itself, unless one happens to find it surprising, but the manner of stating it is witty.

## AIRE AND ANGELS

"Aire and Angels" is perhaps the most complex of all Donne's poems, because of its manner of development, because of its subject, and because of the numerous distinctions of ideas made within a poem of moderate length. Our purpose will be best served by first attempting to make a paraphrase of the poem. It is spoken by a man to a woman. He says that he has loved her before he ever met her, as people worship angels whom they have never seen. It is thus implied that his love was directed toward an idea of a woman, for people have only ideas of angels, never having seen them. When first he met this particular woman, she was a "lovely glorious nothing". That is, she was not yet recognized as the direction or object of his love, or she was not the loved object until he made her so, this being done by his identification of her with his idea of the loved object. The process of identification is thus explained: Love is the child of his soul, and since his soul has taken a body, Love, like the parent, must do so. This it does when it is urged to discover the identity of the woman: it assumes the body of the woman, and in this way the woman becomes the physical referent of what was previously the idea of the loved object. Here the first stanza ends.

The second stanza begins with a conceit by which love is equated with a ship. The speaker of the poem says that in having love assume the body of the woman he thought to have given it stability and fixation—as one ballasts a ship with weight—but he discovers that he has overweighted it. This is explained, after the conceit has been dropped, by the statement that the woman, in all her detail, "for love to worke upon / Is much too much." In other words, it turns out that the woman, as she appears to him, as she represents the ideal object of love, is more than his love can manage to attach itself to. For as his love could not formerly come to rest, when there was no basis on which it might rest, so now it is not able to partake of an extreme and ultimate fulfillment. Consequently, it must abandon this fulfillment of the ideal and adjust itself to the love that the woman offers, not to the woman herself. This adjustment is possible because woman's love is less than man's, and hence can be the "spheare" of man's love, just as an angel's body, though pure, is less pure than the angel's soul contained therein:

> Just such disparitie
> As is twixt Aire and Angells puritie,
> 'Twixt womens love, and mens will ever bee.

So the poem ends.

In approaching a consideration of its structural aspects perhaps it will be well to summarize the paraphrase of the poem: Man has a conception of the woman whom he would love before having found the woman, but when finally an individual woman is accepted as representing this conception, man discovers that his love does not fully measure up to the woman he sees as the loved object, so an adjustment is made according to the measure, not of the woman, but of the woman's love, which is always less than man's.

It is obvious that the poem is not structurally coterminous with a single extended conceit. There is no conceit until the middle of the first stanza, where we have the conceit, extended to the end of the stanza, of love as the child of an embodied soul. Then there is a conceit extended from the beginning of the second stanza through the first four lines, this time of love as a ship that is ballasted. These two conceits are adjacent, but one does not follow the other by logical extension of imagery or even by obvious association; there is a complete break in figurativeness. Their sequence is dependent upon the fact that both are metaphors about love, which is the subject of a discourse that begins before and extends through and beyond both conceits. At the conclusion of the poem there is, not a conceit, but an analogy between the psychological anatomy of angels and the loves of men and of women.

And now let us examine a structural aspect of the poem other than that which would be determined by tropes. According to the paraphrase that was made, the lover addresses the woman he loves in terms of praise, exalting her above himself, until almost the end of the poem. And then it develops that this discussion leads to a statement that the woman is in a respect lower than the lover. With this surprising reversal, seemingly unprepared for, the poem ends. The reversal is surprising, and a calculated surprise is witty. Moreover, the reversal makes for irony: one attitude is apparently prepared for, and then its opposite is given. Hence the poem is not a straightforward development of a single attitude, but provides a complexity of attitudes.

## OTHER POEMS

"Womans Constancy" and "A Valediction: of My Name, in the Window" are poems with a development of structure similar to that of "Aire and Angels". There are still others which contain opposite, and therefore a complexity of, attitudes, but in which the complexity is not established by a sharp reversal at the end of the poem. We find instead, in varying degrees, a complexity of attitudes developed earlier in the poem and with more obvious preparation. And the extent to which such complexity determines the development varies from poem to poem. Sometimes, indeed, a poem begins with the statement of a paradox, and in that case the poem may in no way develop according to the principle we are at present discussing. But the paradox would none the less be a complexity, though this need not be a determining element in the development or structure of the poem.

A feature of "Aire and Angels" making for additional irony and complexity of attitudes is the subject matter. The several aspects of a unit, or individual, are considered as existing independently (somewhat in the manner of faculty psychology); then differing or opposing attitudes are taken toward these aspects, thus making for complexity of attitudes and possibly irony. In "Aire and Angels" there are the lover, his soul, his love, his conception of the woman, the woman, her love. The reversal at the end of this poem is peculiarly dependent upon this division of the individual: it turns from the attitude toward the woman to the attitude toward her love. Complexity of attitude results in other

45

poems having the same use of subject matter: division of the individual into parts and then a separate attitude toward each part. Such poems are "The Undertaking", "Lovers Infinitenesse", "The Broken Heart", "The Extasie", "Loves Diet", and "The Blossome". This complexity is not in a relation to the development or structure of a poem, and irony is not always its concomitant.

## A NOCTURNALL UPON SAINT LUCIES DAY

In the analysis of "Twicknam Garden" it was remarked that "A Nocturnall upon Saint Lucies Day, Being the Shortest Day" is similar to that poem in some distinctive respects. We observed of "Twicknam Garden" that it is peculiarly a dramatic poem, the utterance of a speaker upon a specific situation involving the speaker, and that, in accordance with its dramatic nature, the subject of the poem is the emotion of the speaker. Our method of arriving at this observation was to regard the terms and statements of the poem as references to or reflections of the speaker's emotion, or, in other words, as a characterization of this emotion. And the problem of explicating the "Nocturnall" suggests a similar handling.

The poem opens with the speaker describing an aspect of the situation. The night following the shortest day of the year (St. Lucy's Day, December 22) is coming on, and the speaker sees this longest night as comparable to himself. Winter and profound darkness are upon the world. This condition is described figuratively in negative terms, by what is absent—sap, balm, life—rather than by what is present:

> The worlds whole sap is sunke:
> The generall balme th'hydroptique earth hath drunk,
> Whither, as to the beds-feet, life is shrunke,
> Dead and enterr'd; yet all these seeme to laugh,
> Compar'd with mee, who am their Epitaph.

46

Thus the speaker comments upon himself. The things that are dead and interred are less mournful than he, less negative, for he is the "Epitaph" of these, the very meaning and token of negativity. And such a view of himself implies, of course, the emotion from which the view articulated arises.

In the second and third stanzas the emotion is more fully and more specifically characterized. In addition to the continued stress upon the speaker's feeling of negativity or nothingness, the source and history of this feeling are provided. The speaker addresses himself to those who will be lovers in "the next world, that is, at the next Spring." By this it becomes evident that the emotion has followed from the experience of love. And the speaker goes on to explain what the experience was and how it worked upon him. He advises the lovers to study him, and this advice is apparently a warning to them. In the form of a conceit—the speaker as subject to love's alchemy—he tells of the ultra-nothingness into which he has been made, for he was a kind of nothingness originally:

> For I am every dead thing,
> In whom love wrought new Alchimie,
> For his art did expresse
> A quintessence even from nothingnesse,
> From dull privations, and leane emptinesse:
> He ruin'd mee, and I am re-begot
> Of absence, darknesse, death; things which are not.

The conceit continues into the third stanza, in which it is again said that he is the distillation of nothingness ("by loves limbecke"). And then this original nothingness and the experience of love are further explained, the background, and hence characterization, of the emotion being thus increasingly abundant as the poem develops. Often the speaker and the woman he loved brought themselves to a state of nothingness; they were drowned, or they were chaoses, or carcasses:

47

> Oft a flood
> Have wee two wept, and so
> Drownd the whole world, us two; oft did we grow
> To be two Chaosses, when we did show
> Care to ought else; and often absences
> Withdrew our soules, and made us carcasses.

In the fourth stanza the speaker states precisely what brought him to the condition, or emotion, of which he speaks. This is the death of the woman, by which he is

> Of the first nothing, the Elixer grown.

And he proceeds to describe, negatively, what it is to be this second, more extreme, nothing. Unlike even the most limited objects, he is, since the death of the woman, without the properties of a substance, in no context at all:

> If I an ordinary nothing were,
> As shadow, a light, and body must be here.

The implication of this is that when the woman lived, he was an ordinary nothing, her shadow.

In the fifth and final stanza the speaker reasserts his nothingness and makes a witty contrast between himself and the lovers whom he is addressing. His sun, the woman, will not return, but the other sun will, bringing for the lovers the season of love:

> But I am None; nor will my Sunne renew.
> You lovers, for whose sake, the lesser Sunne
> At this time to the Goat is runne
> To fetch new lust, and give it you,
> Enjoy your summer all;
> Since shee enjoyes her long nights festivall,
> Let mee prepare towards her, and let mee call
> This houre her Vigill, and her Eve, since this
> Both the yeares, and the dayes deep midnight is.

Here, at the end of the poem, the speaker turns from the consideration of his nothingness and the things with which it is contrasted, to the state of the woman and the attitude he will take toward her. Now, instead of construing her death as the event which made him the elixir of nothingness, he will regard it as the event which removed her to bliss, and he will look forward toward his death, by which he will join her in this bliss. Hence the long night is interpreted, not as partially representing his nothingness, but as representing the bliss of her who is dead, the bliss which he anticipates. The hour, symbolic for the death and interment of which he is the epitaph, is also her vigil and eve; it is hallowed for her and in commemoration of her, as it might be by a saint.

So the poem ends, maintaining a complexity of attitudes —or we might here say a tension of attitudes. This complexity consists of the double interpretation put upon the "deep midnight". It is most conveniently illustrated with the expression, "enjoyes her long nights festivall." For here *long night* and *enjoyed festival* are in a combination which includes the two attitudes toward the woman's death: death as it is significant in the mundane and human realm, and death as it initiates the supernatural bliss of Christianity. And as a matter of fact, this complexity, this irony, comes not alone at the end, but exists earlier in the poem: "I am by her death, (which word wrongs her). . . ." There is, moreover, an ironical complexity throughout the poem and at the basis of its most dominant theme. Upon the removal from a situation in which he was already nothing, the speaker becomes steeped in an even greater nothingness. He gives warning to lovers of the future, yet he predicts joy for them and remains himself, in a manner, still attached to the woman whom he loved. He laments his condition, would rather be otherwise in the terms of the world: "I should preferre, / If I were any beast, . . ." Yet he anticipates a joy that is beyond that of the world. His prospect of death is both despairingly suicidal and hopefully optimistic.

Our reading of the "Nocturnall" has shown it to be the

statement of a speaker at a dramatic moment in the speaker's experience. This experience, or plot, is filled out as the poem develops, for the speaker expresses what he feels about the experience. We may say, therefore, that the poem, the speaker's expression, has for its subject the speaker's emotion. With the development of the poem, this emotion is characterized by references to its context and to the complexity of attitudes which constitute it. We may repeat, then, the similarity between the "Nocturnall" and "Twicknam Garden". Both poems are speeches within indicated dramatic situations, and each poem has a dramatic complication beyond its rhetorical complication. That is, all the tropes in the poem (and there are many) with their conceptual burdens, and other kinds of passages also, cohere in a meaningful pattern by dramatic reference, rather than by any figurative device or system of figurative devices. Every element (tropical, conceptual, and perhaps other kinds) is significant in terms of its whole context, while it gives significance to this context; just as every detail of a drama may depend for its meaning upon, and be also part of, the whole drama. Like many other poems of Donne, the "Nocturnall" has several conceits, other witty devices, and a witty, or ironically complex, aspect to its subject; and all of these are present as contributing to the whole organization, or structure, of the poem; none alone, however, is determinant of this organization.

## OTHER POEMS

Once again we may use analyses already made for an economical comment on new poems. There are other poems that are dramatic in the same way as "Twicknam Garden" and the "Nocturnall," each being spoken in a situation clearly indicated and having for subject the emotion of the speaker. Such poems are "The Apparition", "The Relique" and "The Anniversarie". Still others comply with this principle in varying degrees. For instance, in some poems the speaker supplies a discourse on a subject other than his own situation and emotion, not necessarily reflecting an emotion. Or a poem may begin with a specific situation and then develop to the exposition of a generalization, reference being made not to the situation and emotion of the speaker, but to some problem or idea suggested by these. Among such poems are "The Extasie" and "A Lecture upon the Shadow". And there are poems even further removed from any connection with an emotion of the speaker. In these no situation or relationship of the speaker is indicated. Such a poem is written in the first person singular, as "Goe, and catche a falling starre", "Loves Alchymie" and "The Primrose". An opinion is developed, but it is the kind of opinion that is held generally and arises from no particular situation or emotion. These poems are comparable to essays, public statements, as distinguished from dramatic statements that are *private* with respect to the speaker. An account of the speaker's relationship to other materials of the poem would be one way of distinguishing among, grouping, and characterizing the poems of Donne's *Songs and Sonets*; for all of them but two—"Confined Love" and "Communitie"—are *spoken*.

The complexity of attitudes, or the irony, found in the "Nocturnall" is, in its character, illustrative of such complexities as they exist in other poems. In the "Nocturnall" two standards of value are set against each other: death as it is significant in the world, and as it is significant beyond the world. Similarly, in "The Canonization" there are two standards of value: those of the lover and those of the world. In both "The Anniversarie" and "The Relique" the complexity is again derivative of a conflict between worldly values and supernatural values. For instance, in "The Anniversarie" the speaker laments that death must come for the two lovers, though he admits of the happiness which follows death:

51

Alas, as well as other Princes, wee,
(Who Prince enough in one another bee,)
Must leave at last in death, these eyes, and eares,
Oft fed with true oathes, and with sweet salt teares;
　　But soules where nothing dwells but love
(All other thoughts being inmates) then shall prove
This, or a love increased there above,
When bodies to their graves, soules from their graves remove.

In "The Relique" there is a multiple complexity. The speaker contrasts the natural promiscuity of women with his own loved one, who is exceptional in faithfulness and spirituality; and at the same time he would delay the supreme spirituality that there is in heaven:

　　　　When my grave is broke up againe
　　　　Some second ghest to entertaine,
　　　　(For graves have learn'd that woman-head
　　　　To be to more then one a Bed)
　　　　　　And he that digs it, spies
　　　　A bracelet of bright haire about the bone,
　　　　　　Will he not let'us alone,
　　　　And thinke that there a loving couple lies,
　　　　Who thought that this device might be some way
　　　　To make their soules, at the last busie day,
　　　　Meet at this grave, and make a little stay?

Though this kind of complexity may be developed in a poem through the use of conceits, it is not dependent for its presence in the poem upon figurative device. The complexity is, rather, inherent in the ideas, or conceptual content, of the poetry. In each of the poems we have just been discussing there are ideas which, in the tradition of European thought, involve two standards, and these standards are considered as conflicting: there is the world in contrast to the spirituality of love, or there is earthly existence in contrast to supernatural existence.

# A VALEDICTION: FORBIDDING MOURNING

Before finally attempting any generalization drawn from an analysis of Donne's poetry, it appears logical first to take particular notice of those poems that are, or appear to be, coterminous with a single extended metaphor, or conceit, and also of those poems that are in large part so constituted. Such a list may well begin with "A Valediction: Forbidding Mourning", the poem ending with the conceit of the lovers' souls as "twin compasses", perhaps the most famous of all Donne's conceits:

> If they be two, they are two so
> As stiffe twin compasses are two,
> Thy soule the fixt foot, makes no show
> To move, but doth, if the'other doe.
>
> And though it in the center sit,
> Yet when the other far doth rome,
> It leanes, and hearkens after it,
> And growes erect, as that comes home.
>
> Such wilt thou be to mee, who must
> Like th' other foot, obliquely runne;
> Thy firmnes makes my circle just,
> And makes me end, where I begunne.

We discover that, after all, this conceit runs through only the last three stanzas of a poem which is made up of nine stanzas. Though the conceit does not extend through the entire poem, there is a "conceptual burden," shared by this conceit and others, which does so extend. This burden is again, in its most general nature, the complexity of attitudes we have frequently observed elsewhere in Donne's poetry. Two standards of value, or interpretation, are contrasted in the poem: that of the ordinary world, and that of the spirituality of love. This distinction, which is the basic argument of the poem, is stated clearly in the second stanza by the speaker of the poem:

> T'were prophanation of our joyes
> To tell the layetie our love.

In this poem absence between lovers is interpreted by the two standards. According to one of these, when the lovers are absent from each other, a real division results. But according to the other, that of the spirituality of love, the lovers share a single, indivisible soul, and absence has no effect upon this unity, despite appearances. It is this principle which is illustrated in some detail by the conceit of the compasses. We may notice, however, that the principle is already stated in the stanza preceding this illustration, first literally, and then by the simile of beaten gold:

> Our two soules therefore, which are one,
> Though I must goe, endure not yet
> A breach, but an expansion,
> Like gold to ayery thinnesse beate.

Obviously the final conceit does not determine the poem's structure. This conceit, as well as others, may be "important" for a total characterization of the "Valediction: Forbidding Mourning", but if any one element is to be singled out as basic to the whole organization of the poem, and as an element typical among the poems of Donne, it is this theme of complexity of attitudes.

## A FEAVER

The poem "A Feaver" is made up for the most part, though not wholly, of a single conceit. A woman's fever as the conflagration which is destroying the world: this is the metaphor that is extended through five stanzas—that is, through all but the first and last stanzas of the poem. The speaker of the poem addresses this woman, who is dying, and whom he loves. The metaphor says in effect that the woman is a world to the lover. She is, thus, set apart from the ordinary world, and a separate attitude exists for each. Hence, there is in "A Feaver" the typical complexity of attitudes found in many of Donne's poems. We may observe, however, that this complexity is not initiated by the metaphor. It is otherwise stated in the opening stanza of the poem, where the speaker distinguishes between the dying woman and all other women, thus implying that he loves her for some peculiar aspect not pertaining to women in general, but which places her, in a respect, apart from the general class:

> Oh doe not die, for I shall hate
> > All women so, when thou art gone,
> That thee I shall not celebrate,
> > When I remember, thou wast one.

The distinction of the woman, as contrasted to the rest of the world, is reiterated beyond the terms of the conceit. Here are the last two stanzas:

> These burning fits but meteors bee,
> > Whose matter in thee is soone spent.
> Thy beauty,'and all parts, which are thee,
> > Are unchangeable firmament.

> Yet t'was of my minde, seising thee,
> > Though it in thee cannot persever.
> For I had rather owner bee
> > Of thee one houre, then all else ever.

The speaker says that the fever originated in his mind and that it issued to the woman when his mind fastened upon her. He concludes with a reference to the two standards of value, and he affirms one of these, that represented by the woman.

## LOVES DIET

In "Loves Diet", a poem of five stanzas, a single conceit is sustained through all but the last stanza. The nature of the metaphor is implied by the title of the poem. The speaker personifies his experience, or emotion, of love, and he tells of the diet which he forced upon it. The opening stanza will illustrate:

> To what a combersome unwieldinesse
> And burdenous corpulence my love had growne,
>   But that I did, to make it lesse,
>   And keepe it in proportion,
> Give it a diet, made it feed upon
> That which love worst endures, *discretion*.

In the discussion of "Aire and Angels" we have already referred to the complexity of attitudes which exists in this poem. Such complexity, it was observed, results from a division of the individual into several aspects. Then these aspects are considered as existing independently, and one may be opposed to another or to the individual as a whole. An example of this complexity in "Loves Diet" is the opposition of the individual's two impulses, love and discretion. One attitude is represented as being conditioned by other attitudes. This theme continues beyond the conceit of the diet into the final stanza:

> Thus I reclaim'd my buzard love, to flye
> At what, and when, and how, and where I chuse;
>   Now negligent of sport I lye,
>   And now as other Fawkners use,
> I spring a mistresse, sweare, write, sigh and weepe:
> And the game kill'd, or lost, goe talke, and sleepe.

An additional element of this complexity, ironical in character, results from the detachment with which the speaker regards an attitude, as if it were not his own.

## A LECTURE UPON THE SHADOW

At the opening of "A Lecture upon the Shadow" the speaker, addressing a woman, states his intention of making some comment upon the nature of love. First he calls attention to the shadows produced by the couple as they walked together, and to the effect which the course of the sun has upon these shadows. And then, in the form of a metaphor that is extended to the end of the poem, he explains how a complete love is comparable to noon, when the sun is at its highest and shadows are diminished:

> So whilst our infant loves did grow,
> Disguises did, and shadowes, flow,
> From us, and our cares; but, now 'tis not so.

> That love hath not attain'd the high'st degree,
> Which is still diligent lest others see.

The speaker of the poem does not maintain simultaneously a complexity of attitudes. He does indicate, however, that there is such complexity until love has reached its fullest and complete condition. While it has not reached this condition, there are "disguises" and diligence "lest others see." With the conclusion of the poem he insists that there is no complexity in the attitude of love, no intermediate stages or overlapping of attitudes between love and the absence of love:

> Love is a growing, or full constant light;
> And his first minute, after noone, is night.

## LOVES USURY

The poems "Loves Usury", "A Valediction: of the Book", and "The Will" might each be considered as coterminous with a single conceit. Yet these conceits, if they are such, are different in kind from what is typically regarded as an extended metaphor. In the usual conceit there is, as the metaphor is extended, a development of the conceptual burden in terms of the object with which the conceptual burden is equated, and therefore a constant recurrence of figurativeness. But this figurativeness is not to be found in "Loves

Usury". The title of the poem may, indeed, suggest a conceit, or seem to have the potentialities of a conceit, but we do not find in the poem the necessary figurativeness. In fact, any argument for the poem's conceitedness would be less likely if it were not for the title. As we read the poem we find it to be the address of a speaker to Love, the deity. Love is described as "usurious," and reference is made to a "bargain," but the poem develops in terms of experience other than the practice of usury. Here, for example, is the second of the three stanzas which make up the poem:

> Let mee thinke any rivalls letter mine,
> And at next nine
> Keepe midnights promise; mistake by the way
> The maid, and tell the Lady of that delay;
> Onely let mee love none, no, not the sport;
> From country grasse, to comfitures of Court,
> Or cities quelque choses, let report
> My minde transport.

What may in some ways resemble a conceit is really the complication of the conventional myth, love as a god. The statement of a relationship between a man and a mythical god, even though it is a "usurious" yet not financial relationship, is not strictly a metaphorical statement. Possibly it is surprising, but one remembers Mephistopheles and Dr. Faustus.

## A VALEDICTION: OF THE BOOKE

"A Valediction: of the Booke" opens with the declaration, by a speaker to his loved one, that there is a way by which the lovers may "anger destiny"—that is, secure the endless fame of their love and of themselves. This way is explained in the second stanza:

> Study our manuscripts, those Myriades
> Of letters, which have past twixt thee and mee,
> Thence write our Annals, and in them will bee

To all whom loves subliming fire invades,
    Rule and example found;
    There, the faith of any ground
    No schismatique will dare to wound,
    That sees, how Love this grace to us affords,
To make, to keep, to use, to be these his Records.

In the following four stanzas these "Annals" are spoken of
as the book that will provide every kind of learning. Clergy-
men, lawyers, and statesmen will find that it contains in-
formation according to their special needs. In the sixth and
final stanza the speaker says to the woman that she is to
write this book, and that he, going abroad, will study her.
And the poem ends with mathematical, astronomical, and
geographical metaphors to the effect that love is tested by
absence between the lovers. Though an extended metaphor
may have been suggested by the title, we do not really find
one in the poem. In so far as the poem is the *extension* of
anything, it is the extension of the fabulous notion of the
kind of book that may be produced from the lovers' letters.
This fabulous notion is implicitly an affirmation of lovers'
values, and a satire on other kinds of people.


## THE WILL

Because of its title, "The Will" may also give promise of
being a poem coterminous with a single conceit. And it is,
indeed, closer to that condition than "Loves Usury" or "A
Valediction: of the Booke". The poem is addressed to Love
by a speaker who is at the point of death. Throughout the
poem the speaker reveals the details of the legacy he will
leave, and explains them. Thus the poem opens:

    Before I sigh my last gaspe, let me breath,
    Great love, some Legacies; Here I bequeath
    Mine eyes to *Argus*, if mine eyes can see,
    If they be blinde, then Love, I give them thee;

My tongue to Fame; to'Embassadours mine eares;
    To women or the sea, my teares.
  Thou, Love, hast taught mee heretofore
By making mee serve her who'had twenty more,
That I should give to none, but such, as had too much before.

In this manner the speaker lists for five stanzas (all but the last) his gifts and the recipients of his gifts. And in every case the nature of the bestowal consists of a witty incongruity, in illustration of the fact that the woman holds his love as an incongruity, as unacceptable. With the last stanza of the poem the speaker turns from his itemized legacy to a statement of his approaching death, some of the effects it will have, and his purpose in dying:

  Therefore I'll give no more; But I'll undoe
  The world by dying; because love dies too.
    Then all your beauties will bee no more worth
  Then gold in Mines, where none doth draw it forth;
    And all your graces no more use shall have
      Then a Sun dyall in a grave.
    Thou Love taughtst mee, by making mee
  Love her, who doth neglect both mee and thee,
To'invent, and practise this one way, to'annihilate all three.

Since the poem is from beginning to end the speech of a dying man concerning the legacy he leaves, it may appear at first to be coterminous with a single conceit. But unless one considers the statement of an incongruous and absurdly unfeasible gift to be metaphorical, there is really not a single conceit in the poem. The comparisons in the last stanza might possibly be regarded as conceits, but in this stanza there is no longer a recitation of the will.

## THE FLEA

To one who is already preoccupied with the notion of a single extended metaphor, "The Flea" may appear to be so constituted. But it is not really a conceit that is extended through the poem. There is, instead, a maintenance of, or continuous use of, the same witty device. This device is the insistence by the speaker that there is no difference between sexual intercourse and a man and woman being bitten by the same flea; in either case, argues the speaker to the woman, "our two bloods mingled bee." And so the witty, seductive argument continues through the poem. The wit results from the obvious logical fallacy: having sexual intercourse and being bitten by the same flea may be similar in one respect, but not in other respects. When in the second stanza the speaker argues—

> Though parents grudge, and you, w'are met,
> And cloysterd in these living walls of Jet.

his statement is not figurative, but simply false in its implication. This is true also of the final lines of the poem, which the speaker says upon the woman's having killed the flea:

> Just so much honor, when thou yeeld'st to mee,
> Will wast, as this flea's death tooke life from thee.

## A VALEDICTION: OF MY NAME, IN THE WINDOW

Another poem among those which appear to be made up of a single extended metaphor is "A Valediction: of My Name, in the Window". Here the object constantly referred to is, as the title indicates, the name of the speaker cut upon a window; the window is that of the woman he loves. Throughout the poem the speaker tells her to regard this name, during his absence, as representing himself. He states his hope that the name will act as a charm, keeping the woman faithful to him. There are in the poem many metaphors, some of them extended sufficiently to be regarded as conceits. There is not, however, continuous expression of the conceptual burden in the terms of a single metaphor. For instance, though there are some metaphors in the seventh and eighth stanzas, these are not extensions of a single initial metaphor; and the stanzas themselves are a direct statement, from the speaker to the woman, about the fact that his name is cut upon the window. He instructs her in how she is to regard this name:

> So since this name was cut
> When love and griefe their exaltation had,
> No doore 'gainst this names influence shut;
> As much more loving, as more sad,
> 'Twill make thee; and thou shouldst, till I returne,
> Since I die daily, daily mourne.

> When thy inconsiderate hand
> Flings ope this casement, with my trembling name,
> To looke on one, whose wit or land,
> New battry to thy heart may frame,
> Then thinke this name alive, and that thou thus
> In it offendst my Genius.

At the end of the poem, in the eleventh stanza, the speaker turns from the comment upon his name and his hope for faithfulness in the woman, to an observation upon this very comment:

> But glasse, and lines must bee,
> No meanes our firme substantiall love to keepe;
> Neere death inflicts this lethargie,
> And this I murmure in my sleepe;
> Impute this idle talke, to that I goe,
> For dying men talke often so.

It is noteworthy that the final lines of the poem are without any terms that derive from the name or the window. These lines are of special significance, for with them there develops the complexity of attitudes found in many of Donne's poems. The speaker of the poem has been expressing hope because all hope is lost. This is his own conclusion.

# Chapter III

## THE PROBLEMS

### Definitions and Evaluations

W₁ may now draw upon our analyses of poems from Donne's *Songs and Sonets* to make a more final comment on the definitions discussed in the first chapter, and to proceed to generalizations about the poetry which are suggested by our analyses.

### IMAGE, CONCEIT AND STRUCTURE

The extended metaphor, or conceit, appears frequently in the poetry, and would certainly figure in a full characterization of Donne's style. But it is not, we have observed, an element by which the poetry is primarily and essentially characterized. Consequently, it must be concluded that those definitions are not accurate which are based upon the conceit as determining the structure of a metaphysical poem —if we mean that metaphysical poetry is the kind of poetry written by John Donne.

Poems that are coterminous with a single extended metaphor are exceptional rather than representative. Indeed, there is not a single poem in the *Songs and Sonets* which fits exactly the terms of the critic offering this definition. Mr. Ransom, we may recall, declared that there is in metaphysical poetry "a single extended image to bear the whole weight of the conceptual structure."[34] If a physical image is meant, then even such poems as "The Will" and "Loves Usury" could not be considered as examples. We found, moreover, that few images are extended in the terms of imagery; the conceit of the compasses in "A Valediction: Forbidding Mourning" is one of these few. More frequently, however, there are various interpretations of the same image, or there is an accumulation of statements made by reference to a single image. And sometimes a conceit may not originate with a physical image at all, as the conceit of the lovers being canonized in "The Canonization".

These observations apply also to the definition that metaphysical poetry shows a development of imagery by logical extension, as Mr. Tate suggests.[35] In our analyses we did not find that poems are characteristically developed by physical imagery. Though physical images are abundant in the poems of Donne, no one device of a relationship among the images can be singled out as exclusively typical. This definition will not hold even if *imagery* is not interpreted as physical references alone. We may again turn to "The Canonization", this time for an example of the logical development of terms that are not strictly images. The fourth stanza of that poem, we noticed, has a sequence of terms that are allied with each other by obvious association: *legend, verse, sonnets, hymns, canonization.* These terms might be associated with each other even outside their present context; the association of the terms is possible because of their own nature, and not merely because they are used for a particular conceptual development. But there is no reason for regarding this stanza as characterizing or determining the structure of the whole poem. Nor are such examples frequent enough in the poetry to be regarded as the characteristic means by which the poems develop.

We have been saying, in effect, that there is no basis in the *Songs and Sonets* for the statement that a metaphysical poem departs at no point from the manner of the conceit.

64

It will be recalled that the majority of the poems we examined does depart from this manner. And hence, we may say that the conceit is not essentially the "manner" of a metaphysical poem. As we have often observed, the conceit is frequent; and Mr. Brooks is no doubt correct in his contention that the metaphors are not indifferently detachable from a metaphysical poem; but our analysis of the poetry compels us to remark that there is no validity to his dictum: "The comparison *is* the poem in a structural sense".[36] A comparison is often an integral element in the entire complicated structure of a poem, but no justification has been found for generally identifying comparison with the structure of whole poems.

It also follows from our examination of the poems that the conceptual burden is not habitually conveyed by tropes. There are passages in which the conceptual burden *is* thus conveyed. But since such passages are not exclusively typical, there is no basis for saying that the conceptual structure of a metaphysical poem is generally within a figurative structure. A more accurate statement is that tropes are frequently elements in the development of conceptual structure. In other words, the thought abstracted or restated from a passage of metaphysical poetry may or may not be originally expressed by a trope. We noticed, for instance, that conceptual structure develops with slight use of figurative devices in such poems as "Goe, and catche a falling starre", "The Indifferent", "Confined Love" and "Communitie". The obvious structure of "The Prohibition" is conceptual, and this structure is not lost in a prose paraphrase devoid of tropes. Even the condensed and generalized paraphrase of "Aire and Angels" is structurally a closer parallel to the whole poem than is any metaphor or group of metaphors. That is, structure is not generally related to a certain use of metaphor, as the several critics have incorrectly stated it to be. Metaphors and other tropes are often devices for the development of structure, but structure itself is, by figurative standards, looser than such devices. In so far as the structure of an entire poem is in any way determined, it is determined by the sequence of ideas in the poem and the relationship of these ideas to each other. There are, from this point of view, several poems in the *Songs and Sonets* which have a common structure, but we do not find that the poems as a whole yield any single formula of structure that is generally applicable. We do find basis, however, for other kinds of generalization; and hence we can give Donne's poetry a specific characterization, though it will not be structural.

## COMPLEXITY OF ATTITUDES

In the first chapter, while reviewing the modern comment on metaphysical poetry, we observed a striking difference between the characterization given this poetry by Mr. Brooks and that of other critics. He departs from considerations of structure and figurative device. In so doing, he gives an account of the poetry by referring not to the details of technique, but to the attitudes that are expressed in a poem:

Wit is not merely an acute perception of analogies; it is a lively awareness of the fact that the obvious attitude toward a given situation is not the only possible attitude.[37]

There was in Donne's poetry an ambiguity which went far deeper than the mere use of obscure and difficult references. There was—as there is in the case of tragedy—an ambiguity as to the poet's ultimate attitude.[38]

Though we might choose a somewhat different phrasing, description in terms of attitude is, according to our analysis, substantiated by the poems. It will be recalled that most of the poems we examined were found to contain a complexity of attitudes. This complexity may, then, be considered a distinguishing feature of Donne's poetry—and of metaphysical poetry, in so far as Donne's poetry is granted to be the

66

criterion of metaphysical poetry. Although the poems may differ among themselves in varying respects, they do, with few exceptions, have in common the feature of complexity of attitudes.

We have noted how such complexity is specifically constituted. In some poems it consists of references to two standards of value or two standards by which experiences may be interpreted. These standards may be represented thus: the special quality and significance of love, and all other activities and conditions in the world from which love is distinguished. Or the standards may derive from the distinction of human experience and the supernatural experience that follows death. Complexity resulting from the separate attitudes of love and the world is found in "The Good Morrow", "The Canonization", "The Sunne Rising", "A Feaver", "Breake of Day", "A Valediction: of the Booke", "A Valediction: Forbidding Mourning", and other poems. The complexity that derives from human life and the life after death is in "A Nocturnall upon Saint Lucies Day", "The Anniversarie", and "The Relique". These latter poems, it may be noted, contain both kinds of complexity.

There is, as we observed in our analysis of "Aire and Angels", another means by which complexity may exist in a poem. Such complexity results from a conception of the individual as divided into several aspects, thus allowing for differing attitudes toward separate aspects, or even toward the individual and an aspect of the individual—a conception, we remarked, comparable to that of faculty psychology. In "Aire and Angels", for example, there is a distinction between a woman and the woman's love, with a separate attitude toward each. In "Loves Diet" love and discretion coexist independently, and they are also detached from the individual. The heart is given a status separate from the individual in "The Broken Heart", "The Blossoms", "The Legacie", and "The Message". The age-old dualism distinguishing between body and soul is found in "The Undertaking", "The Extasie", and other poems.

A third kind of complexity derives from the conventional psychology of love. Paradoxical or contradictory elements in the experience of love have traditionally been acknowledged. We find, for example, that the lover in "Twicknam Garden" would escape from certain aspects of his condition, but at the same time he would not "leave loving". He laments the falsity of women, and yet he claims to suffer from the "truth" of one woman. In "The Prohibition" the lover would be both loved and hated. At the end of "A Valediction: of My Name, in the Window" the lover says that he has been expressing hope because his case is hopeless.

Having decided that Donne's poetry is generally characterized by complexity of attitudes, we may inquire what is the nature of this complexity. It will be recalled that in every case the attitudes are in relation to specific kinds of human experience, usually the experience of love, sometimes the consideration of death. It appears, then, that a particular subject matter in the poems of Donne makes possible the complexity of attitudes, that the complexity is, indeed, inherent in the subject matter. This subject matter, it will be noticed, is of a kind to which complexity is conventionally attributed. To illustrate this we may simply repeat the different kinds of complexity that were listed: love and the world; human life and the hereafter; love and the other interests or "faculties" of the individual; the paradoxes and contradictions which are the effect of love. This is not to say that the subject of love or death necessarily introduces a complexity of attitudes, or that such complexity is possible only with respect to love and death. Our observation is simply that in the *Songs and Sonets* these subjects, especially love, are exploited for the complexity of attitudes which they imply according to convention. We have seen how in several poems a conventional dualism is treated in various ways, and we may here cite as example a poem not previously discussed. "Breake of Day" is addressed by a woman to her lover after a night together in bed. In the last stanza of the poem the opposition between love and

the world of other activities is made by an analogous reference to matrimonial convention:

> Must businesse thee from hence remove?
> Oh, that's the worst disease of love,
> The poore, the foule, the false, love can
> Admit, but not the busied man.
> He which hath businesse, and makes love, doth doe
> Such wrong, as when a maryed man doth wooe.

Though it will take us beyond the frame of the individual poem, it is not irrelevant to our subject to attempt an
account of poems not containing a complexity of attitudes.
We may notice that these are, after all, in a relationship to
the characteristic common to most of the poems. "Goe, and
catche a falling starre", "Confined Love", and "Communitie" will serve as examples. Readers of these poems might
feel that they are witty or that they incline toward wittiness. The poems, I believe, have the potentiality of wit
because they express attitudes that may be regarded as
extreme. In each of them an opinion is developed, and no
allowance is made for exception to the opinion. In "Goe,
and catche a falling starre" it is insisted that there are absolutely no fair women who are also true. The argument of
"Confined Love" is that women ought to offer themselves
promiscuously. "Communitie" says in effect that men may
use women without moral responsibility because moral issue
is not pertinent to woman. These statements are witty in so
far as they are found surprising, in so far as they violate
conventional attitudes. No wit, or surprise, would result
from an argument that there are exceptions to the idealistic
and romantic convention, that the convention in reality
does not always operate—for the convention does not exist
on such basis. But in these poems the convention is wholly
denied and is usurped by a stringent opposite. They may,
therefore, achieve wittiness by oversimplification, by insisting upon a single attitude toward a question about which a
complexity of attitudes is more generally admitted.

# PATTERNS OF COMPLEXITY

In the analyses of the poems it was noted that there are differences from poem to poem in the way that complexity of attitudes develops or is constituted. An account of these differences is, therefore, suggested.

It may be observed that in some poems, where two separate attitudes are indicated, one attitude is expressed favorably and the other is dismissed, but there is no conflict between the two. We find such relationship of attitudes in "The Good Morrow" and "The Sunne Rising". The world of love is affirmed and maintained and the other world is distinguished from it. This is also to be found in "The Anniversarie", though that poem has an additional complexity arising from the problem of death. In other poems, however, the possibility of conflict, or competition, between the two attitudes is suggested. It will be remembered that the speaker of "The Canonization" insists that one attitude must not impinge upon the other. The speaker of "Break of Day" finds herself the victim of such competition, having to comply with the claims of the unfavored attitude.

In these poems the speaker is committed to one of two attitudes; he does not hold one, and then another. There are poems, however, in which movement from one attitude to another is indicated. For example, the speaker of "The Primrose" considers having for his love one who is either more or less than a woman, and then he decides that it would be best to have a natural woman. The speaker of "Loves Alchymie" observes that in the course of experience one attitude is supplanted by another:

> So, lovers dreame a rich and long delight,
> But get a winter-seeming summers night.

A similar observation is made by the speaker of "A Lecture upon the Shadow". He declares that when love diminishes at all, it has completely ended. In these three poems the attitude to which the speaker may be committed is not so much stressed as it is in poems like "The Good Morrow" and "The Canonization". The speaker of "The Canonization", for example, is involved in a conflict of attitudes; he is a partisan for one of the attitudes. Whereas in "The Primrose", "Loves Alchymie" and "A Lecture upon the Shadow" the speaker delivers a discourse upon attitudes, distinguishing between them, perhaps making a comparative evaluation. He pronounces upon the attitudes in general; but his statement is not initially conditioned by a particular attitude.

There are still other poems in which there is movement from one attitude to another, but in these the movement is not explained in the manner of discourse. The stress is put, rather, upon the speaker's experience of the attitudes as he holds them in a particular situation. Complexity of attitudes is thus developed in "Aire and Angels". Here, we recall, the speaker tells a woman that she fulfills his ideal of love's object; he finds, however, that his love is inadequate for her. But he adjusts his love to the love she offers, for, he says, woman's love is less than man's. Thus he turns from the woman, who is above his love, to her love, which is beneath his. Particularized movement from one attitude to another is illustrated also by "The Prohibition". The speaker cautions a woman about loving him, then about hating him, and finally requests that she love and hate him at the same time. In "A Valediction: of My Name, in the Window" the speaker expresses hope at some length, and then declares that he does this because there is no hope for him. It may be noticed that in these poems there is development *towards* complexity of attitudes; complexity comes as a conclusion. The speaker is, finally, not committed to one attitude alone; nor is he discoursing upon attitudes with any degree of detachment. Though he may at first express—or hold, or seem to hold—a single attitude, it appears in conclusion that he is committed to rival attitudes. Such poems, therefore, arrive at a tension—or at an irony, in that opposite attitudes are held simultaneously by the same individual.

71

A further distinction that may be noted in the relationship between the speaker and the complexity of attitudes is illustrated in "Twicknam Garden" and the "Nocturnall". In these poems the complexity does not issue from a kind of reversal, as it does in "A Valediction: of My Name, in the Window", where surprise may result because the complexity is not admitted until the end of the poem. Instead of development toward a tension or irony, we find that the speaker is from the very first committed to rival attitudes. This was observed in our analyses of "Twicknam Garden" and the "Nocturnall". We indicated their dramatic nature and observed that the emotion of the speaker is in each case the subject of the poem. We referred to this in several ways: a speaker comments upon the specific situation in which he finds himself; the poem is a dramatic statement that is *private* with respect to the speaker; as the poem develops, the speaker's emotion is characterized by references to its context and to its elements; an effect of the poem is this suggestion of the nature of the speaker's emotion. The rival attitudes are, indeed, the specific occasion of the speaker's exclamation. He begins already committed to both attitudes, and as the poem develops we learn of the experience that brought on this rivalry. Hence, it becomes evident that the speaker is in a particular circumstance, a dramatic moment of his experience, much of which is, of course, "inner" experience.

The speaker of "Twicknam Garden" calls himself "selfe traytor". He would escape from what he is experiencing, and yet he would not "leave loving". He deplores the falsity of women, but finds himself distressed by the truth of one of them. Throughout the "Nocturnall" the speaker dwells upon his "nothingness", which is even more profound than the "nothingness" from which it proceeded. He is "nothing" in that he is not committed to anything—or to any one thing. A conflict of attitudes leaves him suspended, each attitude preventing him from being attached to the other. He is "nothing" at the beginning and end of the poem.

The death of the woman he loved has brought him to this condition, yet he says that the word *death* "wrongs her". He would exchange his lot for that of "any beast", yet he anticipates joining his love in heaven. At the particular moment in which he speaks, he inclines in opposite directions but is committed to nothing. In each of these poems, then, the speaker does not discourse upon or expand one attitude and then another, but refers rather to the conflict —the emotion—that he entertains. It appears, therefore, that the conflict of attitudes within the mind of an individual, the individual's emotion, and the dramatic nature of the poem containing these, are the concomitant effects of each other. Such conflict implies an individual's emotion; and it is a dramatic event when an individual expounds the emotion he experiences, especially when the emotion is described in terms of past action and the attitudes toward a present situation.

In reviewing such poems as "The Good Morrow", "The Canonization", "A Lecture upon the Shadow", "Aire and Angels" and "Twicknam Garden", we have observed the different ways in which complexity of attitudes develops, the ways in which attitudes may be related to each other, how the development and relationship of attitudes are connected with the speaker, and finally, how all of these may contribute to the nature of a poem. Though the poems of Donne's *Songs and Sonets* generally have in common a speaker and complexity of attitudes, an obvious conclusion is that there are several patterns by which these details may exist in combination. The patterns that have been indicated should not, however, be regarded as exhaustive. Nor should the distinctions made between patterns be considered as constituting a system of classes into which the poems may be neatly divided. There are poems, no doubt, which fulfill no single pattern, but which show elements of several patterns. Our distinctions were a convenience for indicating the range of configurations in which the common characteristics of the poems may and do exist.

73

# THE CHARACTERISTIC POEM

Since differences among the poems have been defined, questions may arise with regard to the significance of these differences. For instance, one might ask whether any particular poem is, more than another kind, characteristic of the poetry in general. This question might be settled in a way by determining which kind of poem constitutes an emphatic plurality, or perhaps a majority. But such an answer would hardly satisfy what is likely the basic motivation of the question. For one would want to know whether there is a kind of poem, frequent or not, which most essentially displays the common characteristics of the poetry.

To pursue this interest we may examine the characteristics. Do these have an *essential* nature that implies a particular kind of poetic treatment? The poems generally have a speaker and show a complexity of attitudes. One might decide, then, that the poem is most characteristic which displays these most prominently. So the argument would run. Emphasis is put upon the speaker's individuality when he is most clearly the center of a dramatic situation or predicament. And it might be said that complexity of attitudes is most pronounced when the attitudes conflict within the consciousness of a single individual. The notion of complexity does, after all, arise from a mode of consciousness, the single individual's distinction between one attitude and another. Therefore, rivalry of attitudes within the speaker's mind displays most essentially the characteristic of complexity, for the complexity is thus emphasized at its very source. Moreover, such complexity centrally involves the individuality of the speaker. It follows, then, that the speaker's individuality and the rivalry of attitudes may be two aspects of the same pattern of elements, that they converge to produce a poem of dramatic nature. That "Twicknam Garden" and the "Nocturnall" fit this description is undoubtedly apparent. In our treatment of the differences among the poems, it will be recalled, we said of these that "the conflict of attitudes within the mind of an individual, the individual's emotion, and the dramatic nature of the poem containing these, are the concomitant effects of each other." According to such reasoning, it could be maintained that "Twicknam Garden" and the "Nocturnall" represent most fully the prevailing characteristics of Donne's *Songs and Sonets*, that they supply and comply with the essential definition of metaphysical poetry.

But we will soon observe that the special status given to poems of this kind is not really tenable. A similar argument might be made for other kinds of poems. We may, in illustration, consider the kind represented by "Aire and Angels", "The Prohibition", and "A Valediction: of My Name, in the Window", which we discussed as a group. In these, rivalry of attitudes within the mind of the speaker is not apparent until the end of a poem. Each poem shows, in fact, the process by which the speaker arrives at a consciousness of rival attitudes. It might be argued, therefore, that these poems represent the common characteristics more essentially than "Twicknam Garden" and the "Nocturnall"; for, instead of being already possessed of rival attitudes, the speaker reveals in his statement the inceptive stages of the rivalry. While one poem is a statement that issues from a condition of rival attitudes, the other is a statement that is itself the process by which the rivalry develops. This second kind of poem portrays the order of development from the primitive stages to full complexity of attitudes. Such a poem might, then, be regarded as essentially representative of the characteristics; and it has its own claims for dramatic nature.

But as we observed that a special status for "Twicknam Garden" is untenable, so we may now observe that such status is equally untenable for "The Prohibition". Since both kinds show rival attitudes in the mind of the speaker, they might be advanced as sharing the position of being most representative. This implies that conflict of attitudes within the speaker's mind is the most essential instance of complexity; we have just followed arguments in support of this view. There is also an argument for poems in which the speaker does not hold rival attitudes, but is the partisan of a single attitude. Such partisanship distinguishes the individuality of the speaker as much as a conflict of attitudes within his mind, for he thus holds a position in contrast to the one from which he differs. Though he does not maintain a conflict, his statement is an argument for one of two competing attitudes and is thereby dramatic. Complexity is no less essentially represented by an attitude that is held and one that is not held than by any other relationship of attitudes. In either case there is emphasis upon the individuality of the speaker and the complexity of attitudes, and these contribute to a poem of dramatic nature. Poems of this kind are "The Canonization", "A Valediction: Forbidding Mourning", "The Undertaking" and several others. In each of these the speaker maintains the value and spirituality of love against the naturalistic standards of the world.

We may conclude, as a result of these considerations, that no single treatment is most essentially representative of the common characteristics of Donne's poems. It is noticeable, however, that all the poems we have considered are dramatic statements made by the speaker. This still leaves the question of the difference between such poems and those that are discourses. It will be seen that special claims for dramatic treatment of the speaker are not admissible. A poem that is a discourse may attain to dramatic quality by the references that are made, by the obvious particularities to which the general thesis applies. For instance, the speaker of "Loves Alchymie" is in no specified situation at the moment of his statement; in other words, it is not a dramatic statement, but it concerns experiences that are dramatic:

> So, lovers dreame a rich and long delight,
> But get a winter-seeming summers night. . . .

> Hope not for minde in women; at their best
> Sweetnesse and wit, they'are but *Mummy,* possest.

Similarly, the general statement of "A Lecture upon the Shadow" has implications of the particular experience:

> Love is a growing, or full constant light;
> And his first minute, after noone, is night.

"The Apparition" is dramatic not so much by the present situation of the speaker as by the scene he describes and the emotions he predicts. We see, thus, that dramatic quality is not wholly dependent upon the speaker's relationship to the complexity of attitudes, though it may derive from this. In some poems, as a matter of fact, the speaker alternates between references to his own situation and the generalizations illustrated by it, as in "The Extasie". Dramatic quality remains, however, characteristic of the poems. Attitudes presuppose the individuals by which they are held, and by drama we mean, of course, the experience of individuals.

In this attempt to demonstrate that no single treatment of complexity of attitudes is most essential and most dramatic, we have not intended to argue that among the poems of Donne there are no differences in dramatic quality and prominence of complexity. The point of our argument has been that there is no single *formula* for treatment of complexity of attitudes which makes for a poem that is most essentially characteristic or dramatic. We chose particular poems in illustration of several formulas, but do not insist, certainly, that there are no differences among these poems in dramatic quality and the emphasis on complexity. These differences are determined not by the formula, but by the specific treatment of the formula itself. Consider, for example, "The Prohibition" and the "Nocturnall". It is perhaps obvious that a reader would find the "Nocturnall" to be the more dramatic and emphatically complex of the two. But if this is so it is because of the means by which a formula is particularized and not because of a difference in formulas. Or we might consider "The Sunne Rising" and "Breake of Day". Both these poems represent the same formula; and the terms by which it is particularized are, to an extent, strikingly similar, as the titles indicate. Yet "The Sunne Rising" is obviously the more dramatic and essentially complex. The difference must, therefore, result from the peculiar virtues of the individual poems.

## NORMS AND VALUES

The problem of critical evaluation arises, apparently, from this consideration of the several formulas by which an essential complexity of attitudes is possible. Since the same essential complexity and the dramatic quality it may produce are equally possible by all the formulas, differences among the poems other than that of conceptual structure are in no way related to the differences among the formulas. That is, each formula, or norm, is not significant beyond the fact of its descriptive nature; and therefore, no formula may be distinguished from the others as a standard of evaluation. Complexity may be achieved as forcibly by one formula as by another, and since the formulas refer only to the development of complexity, an evaluative function cannot be ascribed to any of them. All are normative descriptions; none is a standard of evaluation. Poems having the same formula of complexity may again be cited in illustration. "The Good Morrow", "Breake of Day", and "The Sunne Rising" all have a speaker who holds the attitude of love as opposed to that of the world. Moreover, the speakers are in identical situations. "The Sunne Rising" would probably be distinguished from the others in superlative terms, and not, obviously, because of any difference in formula. The poems differ in so far as the same formula is differently treated or exploited. And these differences would be stated in terms of the peculiar characteristics of the poems. One might indicate, for example, that "The Sunne Rising" pre-

78

sents most vividly and extensively the elements common to all the poems. One might compare the poems with regard to images, metaphors, diction, tone, concepts, the various interrelationships of all these, and then decide that this poem is the richest, most dramatic, most vivid, most eloquent, most impressive, or use whatever superlatives are suggested by the peculiar nature of the poem.

Since the differences do not depend upon the formula of complexity, poems of different formulas could be compared according to treatment of formulas rather than differences in formulas. If "Twicknam Garden" is a "better" poem than "The Good Morrow", it is so by virtue of the particular details in it which are found preferable to those of "The Good Morrow." "Twicknam Garden" and "The Canonization" might be found equally good. In so far as these poems differ from one another, no single description derived from one could be applied to the other for determining its merit. To the extent that each description is exhaustive, it can refer only to the poem described; and to the extent that it may be applied beyond the poem, it is normative and not evaluative.

It should be remembered that we have been discussing only the poems of Donne's *Songs and Sonets*. We have not referred beyond them to poems that do not have complexity of attitudes by one or another of the formulas. Our conclusions may, however, be so extended, and we may state more generally the distinction between normative description and a standard of evaluation. Several conceptual structures may be used for developing complexity of attitudes, and no one of the structures is for this purpose superior to the others. Unless one puts a special value upon complexity of attitudes—or some comparable feature—there is no conceivable structure that is superior to any other. The terms of superiority would have to derive from the feature or characteristic produced by a particular structure, and the differences in structure would, therefore, be meaningful in terms of this characteristic. And, as we have observed, this implies a special value for a peculiar characteristic. The reasons that one such characteristic should be regarded as more desirable or valuable than another involve the interests of the reader; we shall eventually consider this problem.

In our first chapter we discovered that the structures which have been applied as standards of evaluation were most often rhetorical—or figurative—rather than conceptual structures. That is, metaphysical poetry (and therefore Donne's) was claimed to be distinguished by a structure based upon metaphorical device. But we have demonstrated, presumably, that though metaphor is frequent in Donne's poetry, there is no special use of metaphor by which structure generally develops. We learned that the characteristic structures are conceptual and that metaphor is at times instrumental in the development of these structures. The claims for the special value of a particular metaphorical structure might, consequently, be dismissed.

We should, nevertheless, give these structural standards further consideration. What has been said about conceptual structure is equally true of figurative structure. For example, even if the definition of a metaphysical poem as coterminous with a single extended metaphor were actually borne out by the poetry, there would still be no justification for isolating such structure as absolutely more valuable than any other. It would, like other descriptions, be normative and not evaluative. That is, it would be so unless the extended metaphor were valued *per se* above all other characteristics possible to poetry. But no one, of course, has postulated the extended metaphor as a standard on such unconditional grounds. If it has value, this value must arise from some purpose for which the device is used, and not from the mere presence of the device itself. We may recall Mr. Ransom's statements to the effect that extension of metaphor makes for *meantness* and *precision*. According to his arguments, a poem made of a single extended metaphor is a superior kind of poem:

The impulse to metaphysical poetry . . . consists in committing the feelings in the case . . . to their determination within the elected figure.[39]

"Metaphysics", or miraculism, informs a poetry which is the most original and exciting, and intellectually perhaps the most seasoned, that we know in our literature, and very probably it has few equivalents in other literatures.[40]

The seventeenth-century poets, and especially Donne, may indeed merit extremely high praise. We have already observed, however, that extended metaphor does not necessarily produce any special excellence. It is not demonstrable that the superlative qualities which Mr. Ransom ascribes to the poetry are effected by a single extended metaphor for each poem. Except for the virtue of a conspicuous figurative structure, the excellences of a poem so constituted would derive from the other elements of the poem, not alone from the general formula of structure.

According to our analyses, it is complexity of attitudes which "informs" metaphysical poetry, and no causal relationship between this complexity and extended metaphor is discernible. We have shown that the characteristic complexity exists in poems not distinguished by such figurative device. In "Twicknam Garden" no single metaphor is considerably extended or stands out as most impressive. On the other hand, a single metaphor is extended for twenty lines of "A Feaver". If we compared the two poems we would find this structural difference between them, but the difference would not be significant beyond the fact that it exists. It would certainly not signify a difference in value, or the degree to which the poems are characteristically metaphysical.

The other definitions by which metaphorical device determines the structure of a metaphysical poem, and any claims that such structure is applicable as a standard for general evaluation, are obviously subject to the same arguments we have brought against Mr. Ransom's statements.

It should be clear that the intention of this discussion has not been to disclaim the merit of metaphor, the various poetical purposes for which it may be used, and its importance in the poetry of Donne. Our thesis has been that there is no basis for regarding structure *determined by metaphor* as an absolute standard of evaluation, that Donne's poetry is not generally characterized by such structure.

## METAPHORS AND VALUES

A question of the value of metaphor is suggested by W. R. Moses' interesting study, *The Metaphysical Conceit in the Poems of John Donne.* Following the traditional characterization of the metaphysical conceit as it was first formulated by Dr. Johnson, Mr. Moses describes the conceit as based upon a *discordia concors,* an association of the dissimilar. His treatment of the subject is more systematic than any that has previously been made. He observes that the metaphysical conceit is distinguished for the surprise it produces, the surprise resulting, of course, from the association of dissimilar objects or ideas. To account for the notion of dissimilarity, Mr. Moses avails himself of the term *imaginative category.* In the individual consciousness there are images and ideas which, because of obvious similarity in some details, are associated with each other and therefore comprise separate groups or imaginative categories. Surprise results when terms from different categories are brought into combination. Mr. Moses makes it clear that he is aware of the subjective basis of his terminology:

> . . . an assumption must be made: the assumption, simply, that men are sufficiently alike so that what produces an imaginative shock in one will produce an imaginative shock in most others likewise. This assumption must be understood to operate throughout the present study.[41]

Observing that surprise may result from the degree to which a conceit is extended, as well as from its violation of imaginative categories, Mr. Moses arrives at a standard for the evaluation of conceits:

First, imaginative categories may be alien to each other in varying degree, so that the coupling of terms from disparate categories represents a more or less great deviation from ordinary thought sequences. To use Williamson's expression, "imaginative distance": if a certain quantity of imaginative distance is required to establish a trope as a conceit, there may be, beyond the minimum quantity, more or less distance between the terms of the conceit. Some conceits, accordingly, may produce a great deal of imaginative surprise; others less.

The second cause relates to the "meantness" of the conceit. Terms not imaginatively removed to the farthest possible degree may nevertheless be developed to such an extent that they clash sharply, with a considerable amount of imaginative surprise resulting. But if the conceit is not developed, if the poet does not stick to his imagery, the imaginative surprise produced will (still assuming terms not the farthest removed from each other) be slight. Probably the finest conceits are those characterized both by greatly removed terms and by considerable development.[42]

Though penetrating and cautiously phrased, Mr. Moses' statements are evidently another instance of normative description presented as a standard for general evaluation. Surprise does indeed result from the "coupling of terms from disparate categories". And surprise may, strictly as surprise, be regarded as valuable. But in poetry this is hardly, if ever, the case. There are pleasant surprises, and unpleasant surprises. Unless a reader seeks simply surprise *qua* surprise, he might expect that there be apparent some perceptual—or conceptual—justification for the coupling of disparate terms. Where such justification is not discernible, the surprise would be inconsequential, meaningless, perhaps unpleasant. And the quality of surprise resulting from degree of extension would be similarly determined.

It follows from these observations that the "finest conceit" would not be determined by remoteness of terms or degree of extension. These characteristics are merely descriptive. Where they are of unusual magnitude, we have simply a most conceited conceit, a most surprising surprise. There are, moreover, other factors which participate in the reader's evaluation of a particular conceit, even when the conceit is sufficiently justified. He might be influenced by the perceptual reference made by the terms of a conceit, finding the presence of certain terms—images—especially pleasing. The conceptual burden of the conceit and the way in which this is served by the terms would most likely be even more significant. Consider, for example, this brief conceit from "The Relique":

> (For graves have learn'd that woman-head
> To be to more then one a Bed). . . .

The imaginative distance between graves and beds, and beds and women, is presumably slight. Yet a reader might find this an extremely fine conceit, being much impressed by the references to death and sex, and deeply moved by the nature of the comment on these subjects. Conceptual character is thus seen to be of great importance in the evaluation of a conceit.

Since we are considering conceits in isolation, we might venture a comparison between two conceits. One of these will be the well-known conceit coming at the end of "A Valediction: Forbidding Mourning". Here lovers and compasses are brought together, a large imaginative distance being thus obviously traversed; and the conceit is extended for twelve lines. We may compare with this a conceit from "A Lecture upon the Shadow":

> Love is a growing, or full constant light;
> And his first minute, after noone, is night.

This is of brief extent. The imaginative distances between love and the noon sun, between the absence of love and night, seem less than that between lovers and compasses.

Yet, is one conceit to be regarded as better than the other? There are, indeed, possible reasons for preferring the conceit of the sun above that of the compasses. The comment upon the course of love might be judged as far more impressive than that upon the unity of lovers' souls. It might be argued, moreover, that though one conceit is more extended verbally, the other is compressed and more extended conceptually. A reader might find more intellectual complexity and conceptual implication in the thought that when love passes it does so utterly and not gradually, than in the thought that lovers' souls maintain a kind of unity even when the lovers are parted.

We should again refer to the qualified nature of our argument. It has not been insisted that the determining factor in the value of a conceit is to be found in its paraphrase. We have been concerned simply to show the relevance of the conceptual factor to evaluation, and to repeat that a structural definition is not a standard of evaluation.

It is noteworthy that we have been treating of conceits as they are detached from the poems in which they occur. This suggests an additional means by which the conceit may be evaluated, one that Mr. Moses does not consider. An extremely important basis of evaluation would no doubt be the relationship of a conceit to other elements of a poem and to the whole poem.

It may be observed, upon looking back, that we have discussed several instances of the distinction between description and evaluation. First, we indicated that no single formula for the development of complexity of attitudes is superior to others. Then we showed that poems cannot be evaluated according to a structure that is wholly determined by metaphor. And finally, we decided that the merit of individual metaphors cannot be judged simply by the degree of their extension and the imaginative distance between the terms. In each case a single aspect of structure is selected and is stated generally as a standard of evaluations. Poems may indeed be classified according to one aspect of structure, and metaphors likewise, a common element of style being thus indicated. But, as we have observed, every poem contains many elements in addition to one aspect of structure; these other elements and their relationship to the structural aspect are equally important in determining the value of a particular poem. The value of a poem is not, so to speak, already predicted by the definition of a preconceived characteristic style. It is determinable only in so far as analysis may show a particular poem to have elements that are valuable according to the many interests of a reader.

## READERS AND VALUES

In concluding our study we shall try to give a general account of the value of Donne's poetry, to supply the terms which might be used in explaining its appeal to the reader. Of the elements present in the poems, it is natural to consider first the *complexity of attitudes* which we discovered to be the distinguishing and characteristic feature of Donne's *Songs and Sonets*. This complexity may itself be regarded as a value. It might be so held on the basis that recognition of complexity of attitudes is *realistic*, since life is extremely complex: there are various standards of interpretation that are opposed to each other; individuals seldom share identical attitudes; there are conflicts between the individual and society, and conflicts among the various interests of the same individual. Complexity of attitudes reflects, thus, the actual differences among persons and the psychological nature of the individual. There appears, then, to be a further basis for the value of complexity. It brings into prominence the *psychology of the individual*, which is itself interesting. And the emphasis on human individuality, especially when the individual maintains or is involved in an opposition of attitudes, makes for dramatic quality, which is, like psychology, self-evident in its value. The psychological stress and dramatic quality are, moreover, in conjunction with *the particular subjects of love and death,* and the interest in these is, perhaps, most evident of all.

Though in our analyses we frequently indicated and examined stylistic elements, we did not systematically develop a full account of them. But the existence of these elements and their significance to the reader are no doubt apparent. We may, for example, consider the imagery. Each image is of a particular kind, so we shall assume that the cumulative effect of the images brings the reader to a notion of the general character of the imagery. A reader may, consequently, be interested not only in the presence of imagery, but be pleased to find that it is of a distinguishable kind. And he may, furthermore, be pleased to find it is a peculiar kind—as Donne's imagery may be valued because it is found to be urban, intellectual, realistic.

Other elements similarly participate in meeting the interests of the reader. He may, for instance, like the tone produced by imagery, diction, rhythm, rhyme, stanza; he may like each of these for its own nature and for its contributing function in the development of tone. Donne's tone would, probably, be distinguished and valued because it is conversational, argumentative, and dramatic. Metaphor and other devices may likewise be valued for themselves and because they are instrumental in producing qualities such as surprise, wit, and irony. We observe, then, that an element is not only valued in itself, but for its aptness among other elements. That is, a distinguishable and purposive interrelationship among the elements may be regarded as a value. A reader is pleased by the character of elements that are verbal, figurative, and conceptual; by their discernible integration and the purpose for which they are integrated. In other words, a discernible structure is valuable. It may be so for its character as structure, for its various aspects (i.e., the constituent elements), and for its function in producing the final effect of a whole poem. Though it was not our intention in analyzing his poetry to show its possibilities of value, it may be remembered that we frequently indicated the features we have been discussing. We observed, for example, the various means by which complexity of attitudes is developed and displayed in "The Canonization", "Twicknam Garden", "Aire and Angels", the "Nocturnall", and other poems.

The way in which various elements are involved in a structure may be an additional instance of value. A reader may be favorably impressed by the ingenuity of craft which is reflected by a poem, a craft that was presumably necessary for its creation. Deciding that the deliberate integration of a complexity of elements is no usual and easy accomplishment, he may admire the spectacle of a difficult task successfully performed. He may enjoy, also, his own experience of achieving an understanding of a poem in all its detail. The "difficulty" of a poem would, then, be regarded as a value. A poem may require of a reader some time and effort before the full significance and final coherence of all its elements become apparent. (To ascribe this value, the reader must, of course, first discover significance and coherence, or have confidence that these exist and may eventually be perceived.) A "difficult" poem is, therefore, valuable in that it allows the reader to indulge his own capacities of intelligence and sensibility. Difficulty, whether for the poet or the reader, is admittedly a relative matter. Yet if one considers the concepts underlying Donne's poetry, and the nature of its other ingredient and structural elements, one will probably grant that it is, to a degree, difficult.

These observations certainly do not exhaust the characteristics, or values, of Donne's poetry. And still more certainly, there is no basis for regarding any of these specific values, or any combination of them, as the single absolute standard by which all poetry may be evaluated. If we must have generalizations, they are going to have to be extremely general, such as the proposition that a poem "be about something interesting" and that it show in some way the obvious virtues of unity, coherence and emphasis.

# NOTES

1. H. J. C. Grierson. *Metaphysical Lyrics and Poems of the Seventeenth Century* (Oxford, 1921), p. xiii.

2. *Ibid.*, pp. xv–xvi.

3. T. S. Eliot, *Selected Essays* (New York, 1932), p. 242.

4. T. S. Eliot, "Donne in Our Time", in *A Garland for John Donne* (Cambridge, 1931), p. 16.

5. *Selected Essays*, p. 246.

6. *Ibid.*, p. 247.

7. *Ibid.*, p. 252.

8. George Williamson, *The Donne Tradition* (Cambridge, 1930), p. 29.

9. *Ibid.*, pp. 31–32.

10. *Ibid.*, pp. 22–23.

11. *Ibid.*, p. 34.

12. *Ibid.*, p. 84.

13. John Crowe Ransom, *The World's Body* (New York, 1938), p. 135.

14. *Ibid.*, pp. 141–42.

15. *Ibid.*, p. 136.

16. *Ibid.*, p. 137.

17. *Ibid.*, p. 286.

18. John Crowe Ransom, "Honey and Gall", *Southern Review*, VI (1940), 10.

19. John Crowe Ransom, *God without Thunder* (New York, 1930).

20. *The World's Body*, p. 42.

21. *Ibid.*, p. 348.

22. Allen Tate, "A Note on Donne", *On the Limits of Poetry* (New York, 1948), p. 331.

23. "Tension in Poetry", *Ibid.*, p. 80.

24. *Ibid.*, p. 86.

25. Cleanth Brooks, *Modern Poetry and the Tradition* (Chapel Hill, 1939), p. 15.

26. *Ibid.*, p. 39.

27. *Ibid.*, p. 37.

28. *Ibid.*, p. 43.

29. *Ibid.*, p. 60.

30. *Ibid.*, p. 66.

31. John Crowe Ransom, "Apologia for Modernism", *Kenyon Review*, II (1940), 249.

32. Brooks, *op. cit.*, p. 61.
33. *Ibid.*, p. 209.
34. "Honey and Gall", *loc. cit.*, p. 10.
35. "Tension in Poetry", *loc. cit.*, p. 106.
36. *Op. cit.*, p. 15.
37. *Op. cit.*, p. 37.
38. *Ibid.*, p. 209.
39. *The World's Body*, p. 286.
40. *Ibid.*, p. 135.
41. W. R. Moses, *The Metaphysical Conceit in the Poems of John Donne;* unpublished dissertation (Vanderbilt University Library, 1938), p. 39.
42. *Ibid.*, pp. 101–102.

# BIBLIOGRAPHY

Brooks, Cleanth. *Modern Poetry and the Tradition*. Chapel Hill, University of North Carolina Press, 1939.

Donne, John. *Poems:* ed. Sir H. J. C. Grierson. London, Oxford University Press, 1933.

Eliot, T. S. "Donne in our Time", in *A Garland for John Donne*, ed. Theodore Spencer. Cambridge, Harvard University Press, 1931.

Eliot, T. S. *Selected Essays, 1917–1932*. New York, Harcourt, Brace, 1932.

Grierson, Sir H. J. C. (ed.). *Metaphysical Lyrics and Poems of the Seventeenth Century*. Oxford, Clarendon Press, 1921.

Moses, W. R. *The Metaphysical Conceit in the Poems of John Donne;* Unpublished dissertation, Vanderbilt University Library, 1938.

Ransom, John Crowe, "Apologia for Modernism", *The Kenyon Review*, II (1940), 247–51.

Ransom, John Crowe. *God without Thunder, An Unorthodox Defense of Orthodoxy*. New York, Harcourt, Brace, 1930.

Ransom, John Crowe. "Honey and Gall", *The Southern Review*, VI (1940), 2–19.

Ransom, John Crowe. *The World's Body*. New York, Charles Scribner's Sons, 1938.

Tate, Allen. *On the Limits of Poetry*. New York, The Swallow Press & William Morrow, 1948.

Tuve, Rosemond. *Elizabethan and Metaphysical Imagery*. Chicago, University of Chicago Press, 1947.

Williamson, George. *The Donne Tradition*. Cambridge, Harvard University Press, 1930.